WILD ANIMAL KNITS

**Also by Melinda Coss
and published by Cassell:**
Art Deco Knits (1990)

WILD
ANIMAL
KNITS

MELINDA COSS

CASSELL

I dedicate this book to Ruth,
For thirty years my friend.
Through fire, famine, feast and flood,
Stood by me to the end.

A CASSELL BOOK

First published in the UK
1994 by Cassell
Villiers House
41/47 Strand
London
WC2N 5JE

The line illustrations in the 'Techniques' chapter are by Kate Simunek.

Distributed in Australia
by Capricorn Link (Australia) Ltd
2/13 Carrington Road, Castle Hill, NSW 2154

British Library Cataloguing-in-Publication Data
Coss, Melinda
  Wild Animal Knits
  1. Knitting. Animal motifs
  I.   Title
  746.43'2

ISBN   0-304-34134-7
           0-304-34237-8 (paperback)

Typeset by Litho Link Ltd, Welshpool, Powys, Wales

Printed and bound in Hong Kong by Dah Hua Printing Co Ltd.

CONTENTS

ABBREVIATIONS

alt	alternate
beg	beginning
cb6	slip 3 sts on to a cable needle and hold at back of work, k3, knit 3 from cable needle
cf6	slip 3 sts on to a cable needle and hold at front of work, k3, knit 3 from cable needle
cm	centimetre(s)
cont	continue
dec	decrease
in	inch(es)
inc	increase
k	knit
k2 tog	knit 2 stitches together
k1 tbl	knit 1 through back loop
moss st	k1, p1, repeat to end; on return row, purl the knit stitches and knit the purl stitches
p	purl
p2 tog	purl 2 stitches together
psso	pass slip stitch over
rem	remaining
rep	repeat
RS	right side
sl 1	slip 1 stitch
sl st	slip stitch
st(s)	stitch(es)
st st	stocking stitch
tog	together
WS	wrong side
yrn	wrap yarn once round needle

TECHNIQUES

READING THE CHARTS

Throughout the book explanatory charts show the colour designs charted out, with stitch symbols added where necessary. Each square represents one stitch across – i.e., horizontally – and one row up – i.e., vertically. The charts should be used in conjunction with the written instructions, which will tell you where and when to incorporate them. Any colours required or symbols used will be explained in the key. Always assume that you are working in stocking stitch unless otherwise instructed.

If you are not experienced in the use of charts, remember that when you look at the flat page you are simply looking at a graphic representation of the right side of your piece of work – i.e., the smooth side of stocking stitch. For this reason, the charts begin with a right side (RS) row so that you will be able to see exactly what is going on as you knit. Knit rows are worked from right to left and purl rows from left to right, unless otherwise stated.

TENSION

Knitting is simply a series of connecting loops, the construction of which is totally under the knitter's control. Tension is the term used to describe the actual stitch size – its width regulating the stitch tension measurement and its depth regulating the row tension measurement. Obtaining a specific tension is not a magical skill denied to all those but the initiated. It is a technicality, and the controlling factor is the size of needles used by the knitter.

Since all knitting instructions are drafted to size using mathematical calculations relating to one tension and one tension only, that tension must be achieved before you start the work or you will have no control whatsoever over the size of the finished garment. *This is the most important rule of knitting.*

At the beginning of every pattern, a tension measurement will be given, using a specific stitch and needle size – e.g., 'using size 5mm needles and measured over st st, 18 sts and 24 rows = 10cm (4in) square'. You must work a sample using exactly the same stitch and needle size as quoted. Cast on the specified number of stitches plus at least two extra because edge stitches will not be counted as they do not give an accurate measurement. When it is complete, lay the tension sample or 'swatch' on a flat surface and, taking great care not to squash or stretch it, measure the tension, using a ruler and pins. A fluffy yarn such as mohair can make individual stitches very difficult to see, especially with the darker colours. A handy hint is to hold the swatch up to the light so that the stitches may be clearly distinguished, place the pins either side of the required number of stitches and then lay it down for measuring.

If there are too few stitches, your tension is too loose. Use needles that are one size smaller to work another swatch. If there are too many stitches, your tension is too tight. Use needles that are one size larger to work another swatch.

Even if you have to change needle sizes several times, *keep working swatches until you get it right.* You save no time by skipping this stage of the work because if you do so, you risk having to undo an entire garment that has worked out to the wrong size. You may feel that a slight difference is negligible, but a tension measurement that is only a fraction of a stitch out per centimetre will result in inaccurate sizing because each fraction will have been multiplied by the number of centimetres across the work.

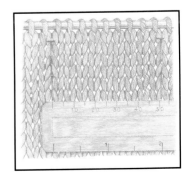

Use a ruler and pins to measure the tension of a sample piece of knitting.

TECHNIQUES

If you have had to change your needle size to achieve the correct tension for the main stitch, and if other parts of the garment are worked on different sized needles, these must also be adjusted by the same ratio. For example, if you are using needles that are one size smaller than are quoted for stocking stitch, you must use needles that are one size smaller than are quoted for the ribbing.

I have intentionally omitted detailed reference to row tension because many people worry over this unnecessarily, changing their needle size even though they have achieved the correct stitch tension. Although it is important, row tension does vary considerably from yarn to yarn and from knitter to knitter. If your stitch tension is absolutely accurate, your row tension will be only slightly out. Nevertheless, keep an eye on your work, especially when you are working something like a sleeve that has been calculated in rows rather than centimetres, and compare it with the measurement chart in case it becomes noticeably longer or shorter.

FAIR ISLE

The technique of colour knitting called 'Fair Isle' is often confused with the traditional style of colour knitting that originated in the Fair Isles and took its name from there. Knitting instructions that call for the Fair Isle method do not necessarily produce a small-motifed repetitive pattern, as sported by the Prince of Wales in the 1920s – far from it, as can be seen from some of the patterns in this book.

The method referred to as Fair Isle knitting is when two colours are used across a row, with the one not in use being carried at the back of the work until it is next required. This is normally done by dropping one colour and picking up the other, using the right hand. If you are lucky enough to have mastered both the 'English' and 'Continental' methods of knitting, each yarn may be held simultaneously, one in the left hand, the other in the right hand. The instructions below, however, are limited to the more standard one-handed method and give the three alternative methods of dealing with the yarn not in use.

STRANDING

Stranding is the term used to describe the technique by which the yarn not in use is simply left hanging at the back of the work until it is next needed. The yarn in use is then dropped and the carried yarn taken up, ready for action. This means that the strand, or 'float', thus produced on the wrong side of the work pulls directly on the stitches either side of it.

It is essential to leave a float long enough to span this gap without pulling the stitches out of shape and to allow the stitches in front of it to stretch and not to pucker on the right side of the work. It is preferable to go to the other extreme and leave a small loop at the back of the work rather than pull the float too tightly.

If the gap to be bridged by the float is wide, the strands produced may easily be caught and pulled when putting the garment on or taking it off. This may be remedied by catching the floats down with a few stitches on the wrong side of the work when you are making up the garment.

WEAVING

With this method the yarn being carried is looped over or under the working yarn on every stitch, creating an up and down woven effect on the wrong side of the work. Since the knitter does not have to gauge the length of the floats, many people find that this is the easiest method of ensuring an even, accurate tension. Weaving does increase the chances

The wrong side of the work showing stranding at the correct tension.

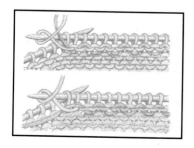

The wrong side of weaving, showing the up and down path of the carried yarn.

TECHNIQUES

of the carried colour showing through on the right side of the work, however, and it tends to produce a far denser fabric, which is not always desirable when a thick, warm fibre such as mohair is being used.

STRANDING AND WEAVING

Combining the two methods of stranding and weaving is invariably the most practical solution to the problem of working perfect Fair Isle. Most designs will have colour areas that will vary in the number of stitches. If the gap between areas of the same colour is only a few stitches then stranding will suffice, but if the float produced will be too long, weave in the carried yarn every few stitches. Should you be unsure about the length of float to leave, slip a finger under one. If you succeed with ease, the float is too long.

The most difficult aspect of Fair Isle knitting is getting the tension correct. This does not depend on the stitch size so much as on the way you treat the carried yarn. This is why, when working an all-over Fair Isle pattern, you should always knit a tension sample in Fair Isle, not in base colour stocking stitch, as the weaving or stranding will greatly affect the finished measurement of the stitches. The most important rule to remember is that *the yarn being carried must be woven or stranded loosely enough to have the same degree of 'give' as the knitting itself.* Unless this is achieved, the resulting fabric will have no elasticity whatsoever; in extreme examples very tight floats will buckle the stitches so that they lie badly on the right side of the work.

If you are working a colour motif using the Fair Isle technique on a single-colour background, keep the tension of the motif as close as possible to the background tension. If there is a great difference, the motif stitches will distort the overall image.

INTARSIA

Intarsia is the term used for the technique of colour knitting whereby each area of colour is worked using a separate ball of yarn, rather than carrying yarns from one area to another as in the Fair Isle technique. Any design that involves large blocks of isolated colour that are not going to be repeated along a row or required again a few rows later should be worked in this way.

There are no limitations to the number of colours that may be used on any one row, other than those imposed by lack of patience and/or dexterity. Avoid getting into a tangle with too many separate balls of yarn hanging from the back of the work, and remember that every time a new ball of yarn is introduced and broken off after use, two extra ends are produced that will have to be secured at the end of the day. When ends are left, always make sure that they are long enough to thread up so that they may be properly fastened with a pointed tapestry needle. Do this very carefully through the backs of the worked stitches so as not to distort the design on the right side of the work. The ends that are left should never be knotted because they will make the wrong side of the work look extremely unsightly. As well as this, they will invariably work themselves loose and create problems at a later stage.

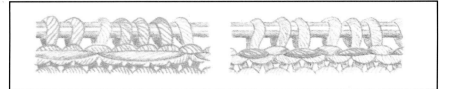

Stranding and weaving worked too tightly.

If you are using the intarsia method, twist the yarns firmly together when you change colours.

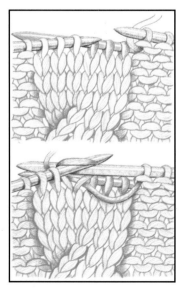

The front cross cable.

If only a few large, regular areas of colour are being worked, then, to avoid any tangling of the wool, lay the different balls of yarn on a table in front of you or keep them separate in individual jam jars or shoe-boxes. However, this requires careful turning at the end of every row so that the various strands do not become twisted.

The easiest method of all is to use small bobbins that hold each yarn separately and that hang at the back of the work. These are available at most haberdashers or department stores or may be made at home out of stiff card. They come in a variety of shapes, but all have a narrow slit in them that keeps the wound yarn in place but allows the knitter to unwind a controlled amount as and when required. When winding yarn on to a bobbin, try to wind sufficient to complete an entire area of colour, but do not overwind because heavy bobbins may pull stitches out of shape.

When actually changing colour from one stitch to another, it is vital that you twist the yarns around one another before dropping the old colour and working the first stitch in the new colour. This prevents a hole from forming. If it is not done, there is no strand to connect the last stitch worked in the first colour to the first stitch worked in the second colour. This twisting should also be done quite firmly to prevent a gap from appearing after the work has settled.

CABLES

A basic cable is simply a twist in the knitted fabric caused by working a small number of stitches out of sequence every few rows. This is done by slipping the stitches on to a needle and leaving them at the front or the back of the work while the next stitches on the left-hand needle are worked. The held stitches are then worked normally.

The cable, worked in stocking stitch, will invariably be flanked by a few reversed stocking stitches in order to give it definition. Since it does involve a twist, however, a cabled fabric will always have a tighter tension than one worked in plain stocking stitch, so take extra care when working your tension sample.

Cable needles are very short and double-pointed. Some have a little kink in them to help keep the stitches in place while others are being worked. Use one that is a similar size to the needles being used for the main work and take care not to stretch or twist the stitches when you are moving them from needle to needle.

On the right side of the work, if the stitches are held to the front, the cable will cross from the right to the left. If the stitches are held at the back of the work, the cable will twist from the left to the right.

FRONT CROSS CABLE

1 (RS): Work to the six stitches that are to be cabled. Slip the next three stitches on the left-hand needle on to the cable needle and leave them hanging at the front of the work.
2 Knit the next three stitches on the left-hand needle as normal.
3 Knit the three held stitches off the cable needle.

Repeat this twist wherever indicated in the instructions.

SEAMS

After achieving the correct tension, the final sewing up of your knitting is the most important technique to master. It can make or break a garment, however carefully it may have been knitted. This is why the making up

TECHNIQUES

instructions after every set of knitting instructions should be followed to the letter, with particular reference to the type of seam and the order in which the seams are to be worked.

Before you start any piece of work, always leave an end of yarn long enough to complete a substantial section of the eventual seam, if not the whole thing. After working a couple of rows, wind this up and pin it to the work to keep it out of the way. If required, also leave a sizeable end when the work has been completed. This saves having to join in new ends, which may well work loose, especially at stress points, such as under the arms or a neckline.

The secret of perfect-looking seams is uniformity and regularity of stitch. When joining two pieces that have been worked in the same stitch, they should be joined row for row and all work should be pinned first to ensure an even distribution of fabrics. When joining work that has a design on both pieces, take great care to match the colours, changing the colour you are using to sew the seam where necessary.

BACKSTITCH

Pin the two pieces of work together, right sides facing, making sure that the edges are absolutely flush. Always leave as narrow a seam allowance as possible to reduce unnecessary bulk. It is essential that the line of backstitches is kept straight, using the lines of the knitted stitches as a guide. Each stitch should be identical in length, one starting immediately after the previous one has finished. On the side of the work facing you this should form a continuous, straight line. If the seam is starting at the very edge of the work, close the edges with an overstitch. Now work the backstitch as follows.

1 Make a running stitch (maximum length 1cm (½in)) through both thicknesses of work.
2 Put the needle back into the work in exactly the same spot as before and make another running stitch twice as long.
3 Put the needle back into the work adjacent to the point where the previous stitch ended. Make another stitch the same length.

Keep repeating step 3 until the last stitch, which needs to be half as long to fill in the final gap left at the end of the seam.

By keeping the stitch line straight and by pulling the yarn fairly firmly after each stitch, no gaps should appear when the work is opened out and the seam pulled apart.

This seam is suitable for lightweight yarns or where an untidy selvedge has been worked.

FLAT SEAM

This seam is a slight contradiction in terms since its working involves an oversewing action, but when the work is opened out it will do so completely and lie quite flat, unlike a backstitched seam.

A blunt-ended tapestry needle should be used to avoid splitting the knitted stitches. Pin both pieces with the right sides together. The needle is placed through the very edge stitch on the back piece and then through the very edge stitch on the front piece. The yarn is pulled through and the action repeated. Always place the needle through exactly the same part of each stitch every time and always work through the edge stitch only. By taking in more than this, a lumpy, untidy seam will be produced that will never lie flat.

When two pieces of stocking stitch are to be

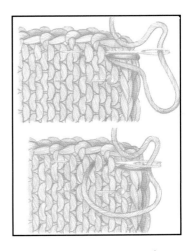

If you use backstitch to join a seam and you are starting at the very edge of the work, close the edges with an overstitch before beginning the row of backstitch.

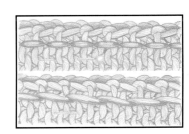

When you use backstitch to join a seam, the finished seam should be perfectly straight; the diagrams illustrate the appearance of the front (top) and back (below) of the completed seam.

TECHNIQUES

The diagrams show how you should hold the knitting to work a flat seam and how the work will look on the right side.

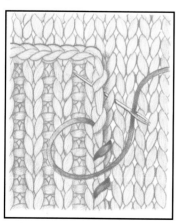

Use slip stitch to attach a pocket to a garment.

joined with a flat seam, do not work any special selvedge, such as knitting every edge stitch. Just work the edge stitches normally but as tightly as possible, using only the tip of your needle. When you come to work the seam, place the needle behind the knots of the edge stitches and not the looser strands that run between the knots since these will not provide a firm enough base for the seam, which will appear gappy when opened out.

Flat seams are essential for heavy-weight yarns where a backstitch would create far too much bulk. They should also be used for attaching buttonbands, collars and so on where flatness and neatness are essential.

Borders, waistbands, cuffs and any other part of a garment where the edge of the seam will be visible should be joined with a flat seam, even if the remainder of the garment is to have a backstitched seam. Start with a flat seam until the rib/border is complete and then change over to a backstitch, taking in a tiny seam allowance at first and then smoothly widening it without making a sudden inroad into the work.

SLIP STITCH

Where one piece of work is to be placed on top of another – when you are turning in a double neckband, folding over a hem or attaching the edges of pocket borders, for example – slip stitch should be used.

When you are turning in a neckband that has been cast off, the needle should be placed through the cast-off edge and then through the exact same stitch but on the row where it was initially knitted up. It is essential to follow the line of the stitch in this way to avoid twisting the neckband. By repeating the action, the visible sewn stitch runs at a diagonal.

The same rule applies when sewing down a neckband that has not been cast off but that has had its stitches held on a thread. The only difference is that the needle is placed through the actual held stitch, thus securing it. When each stitch has been slip-stitched down, the thread may be removed. This method allows for a neckband with more 'give' than one that has been cast off.

On pocket borders use the line of stitches on the main work as a guide to produce a perfectly straight vertical line of stitches. Place the needle through one strand of the main work stitch and then behind the knot of the border edge stitch, as for a flat seam.

KNITTED SHOULDER SEAMS

This method of joining is perfect for shoulders on which no shaping has been worked or on which the shaping has been achieved by working short rows. It creates an extremely neat, flat seam.

Since the two pieces to be joined must be worked stitch for stitch, they must both have exactly the same number of stitches. Even though the pattern specifies that you should have a certain number of stitches at this point, it is wise to double check the number you actually have on your needles since it is very easy to lose or gain the odd stitch accidentally along the way.

The technique itself involves the use of three needles. The stitches from the front and back are held on their respective needles, both in the left hand, while the right hand holds a third, larger, needle which helps to prevent the cast-off stitches from becoming too tight. Holding more than one needle in the hand and trying to work through two stitches at a time without dropping them can seem very awkward at first, but with a little practice it

TECHNIQUES

will feel like normal knitting.

The needles are held with the right sides of the work facing one another and with the stitches lined up at corresponding intervals on the front and back needles.

1 The point of the right-hand needle is put through the first stitch on the front needle and the first stitch on the back needle, with exactly the same action as a regular knit stitch but going through both simultaneously.

2 Pull a loop through to form a single stitch on the right-hand needle, the old stitches being slipped off the left-hand needle.

3 Steps 1 and 2 are repeated so that there are two stitches on the right-hand needle. The second stitch is then lifted over the first, as in regular casting off.

Step 3 should be repeated across all the stitches to be knitted together until one loop remains on the right-hand needle. Pull the yarn through this to secure it.

When you are knitting together a shoulder seam on a garment where no neck shaping has been worked and the neck stitches have not been cast off, all the stitches on the back may be dealt with at the same time. By starting to work the first shoulder together from the armhole to the neck edge, the back neck stitches may then be cast off (if the pattern requires that they are cast off), without breaking the yarn, which may then be used to knit together the second shoulder seam.

Normally worked on the inside of the work to create an extremely neat, flat and durable seam on the right side of the work, a knitted seam may be worked with the wrong sides of the knitting facing one another. This creates a decorative ridge on the right side of the work.

EMBROIDERY

When working figurative motifs, it is not always possible to create a detailed, accurate picture using knitting alone, since you are always ruled by the size and structure of the stitch itself. The addition of embroidery gives that much more flexibility. A small backstitch is the most useful one for creating a single line. It is used in three of the designs in this book – A Giraffe Called Daisy, Culture Vulture and One Hump or Two? Work backstitch as described under Seams.

Satin stitch is used to work the giraffe's nose in A Giraffe Called Daisy. Working from left to right, you should bring the yarn through to the lower edge of the shape you want to fill and insert your needle into the opposite edge. Bring out your needle again close to the point from which the first stitch was made and insert it again close to the first stitch on the opposite edge. Continue in this way until you have completely covered the area with smooth, evenly spaced stitches.

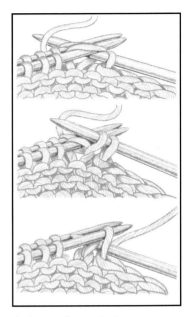

The diagrams illustrate the three steps involved in knitting shoulder seams together. You must always have exactly the same number of stitches on the two pieces that are to be joined in this way.

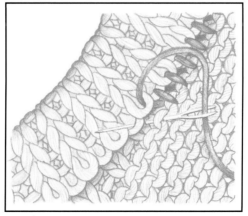

Use slip stitch to hold a double neckband in position.

TIGER LILY

A tiger skin bat-wing jumper and matching coat worked in stocking stitch using the intarsia method (see Techniques). The jumper will fit chest size 86-102cm (34-40in).

MATERIALS

Jumper

Melinda Coss Mohair – 400gm black; 100gm yellow; 150gm mink.

Coat

Melinda Coss Mohair – 400 gm black; 200gm yellow; 150gm mink. 9 buttons, 2.5cm (1in) in diameter.

NEEDLES

One pair of 4½mm and one pair of 5½mm needles; one long circular 5½mm needle. Stitch holders.

TENSION

Using 5½mm needles and measured over st st, 16 sts and 21 rows = 10cm (4in) square.

JUMPER

FRONT

Using 4½mm needles and black, cast on 93 sts. Work in k1, p1 rib as follows:

Row 1 (RS): k1, *p1, k1. Rep from * to end.

Row 2: p1 *k1, p1. Rep from * to end.

Rep the last 2 rows until rib measures 20cm (8in), and inc 9 sts evenly across the last row of rib (102 sts).

Change to 5½ mm needles and begin working from chart.

NB The chart shows half the front or back with increases for half of the sleeve. Work the chart from right to left in knit, then cont to work across the same row in knit but reading the chart from left to right, thus making the second half the mirror image of the first half.

Next row (WS): using purl throughout this row, work the chart reading from right to left, then cont the row in purl but reading the chart from left to right. Cont following the chart in this way, inc 1 st at each end of every 4th row 11 times, then every 3rd row twice, then every alt row 6 times. (When you feel you have too many sts for your straight needles, transfer to a circular needle but cont working backwards and forwards as set.) Cast on 2 sts at beg of every row 14 times, then cast on 3 sts at beg of every row 12 times (204 sts). Cont with further shaping until 110 rows have been worked from start of chart.

Shape neck. (RS): k84, turn and leave remaining sts on a spare needle. Working on this first set of sts only, dec 1 st at neck edge on next and following 5 rows. Complete chart and leave remaining sts on a spare needle. With RS facing, slip centre 36 sts on to a

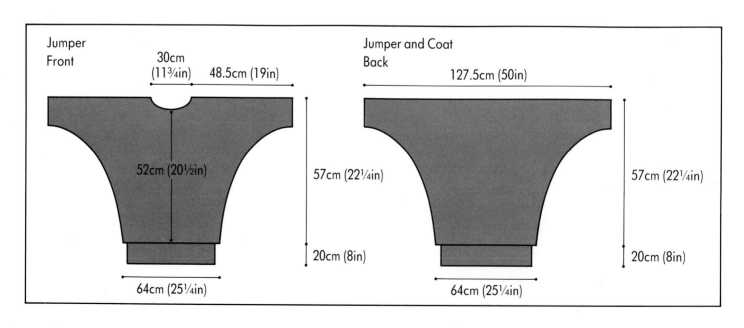

Jumper Front

30cm (11¾in)   48.5cm (19in)

52cm (20½in)

57cm (22¼in)

20cm (8in)

64cm (25¼in)

Jumper and Coat Back

127.5cm (50in)

57cm (22¼in)

20cm (8in)

64cm (25¼in)

TIGER LILY

holder for front neck. Rejoin yarn and work to end of row.
Shape second side to match first side. Leave remaining sts on a spare needle.

BACK
Work as for front but omit neck shaping. When chart is complete, leave sts on circular needle, placing a marker 78 sts in at each end, thus marking 48 sts for centre back neck.

COLLAR
With RSs of back and front facing, knit right shoulder seam together, using colours as set in the design. With RS facing, using 4½mm needles and black, pick up and knit 12 sts down neck shaping, pick up and inc to 66 sts evenly across front stitch holder, pick up and knit 12 sts up second neck shaping, pick up and inc to 82 sts evenly across centre 48 sts of back neck (172 sts). Work in k1, p1 rib as given for front, starting with a row 2. Rib for 18cm (7¼in), finishing with a row 2. Cast off loosely in rib. Knit second shoulder seam together, then join collar seam, reversing seam halfway down for turnback.

CUFFS
Using 4½mm needles, black and with RS facing, pick up and knit 54 sts across base of sleeve.
Next row: p2, *p2 tog, p2, rep from * to last 4 sts, p2 tog, p2 (41 sts). Cont in k1, p1 rib as given for front, starting with a row 1. Rib for 10cm (4in), finishing with a row 2. Cast off in rib. Join side, sleeve and cuff seams in black.

COAT

LEFT FRONT
Using 4½mm needles and black, cast on 51 sts. Work in k1, p1 rib as for back until rib measures 20cm (8in).
Change to 5½mm needles and begin working from chart in st st, inc 1 st at end of every

4th row 11 times, then inc 1 st at same edge of every 3rd row twice, then every alt row 6 times. Cast on 2 sts at end (shaped edge) of every alt row 7 times, then cast on 3 sts at end of every alt row 6 times (102 sts). Cont without further shaping until 110 rows have been

'Tiger Lily'
Big cowl mohair jumper and matching coat in tiger print.

TIGER LILY

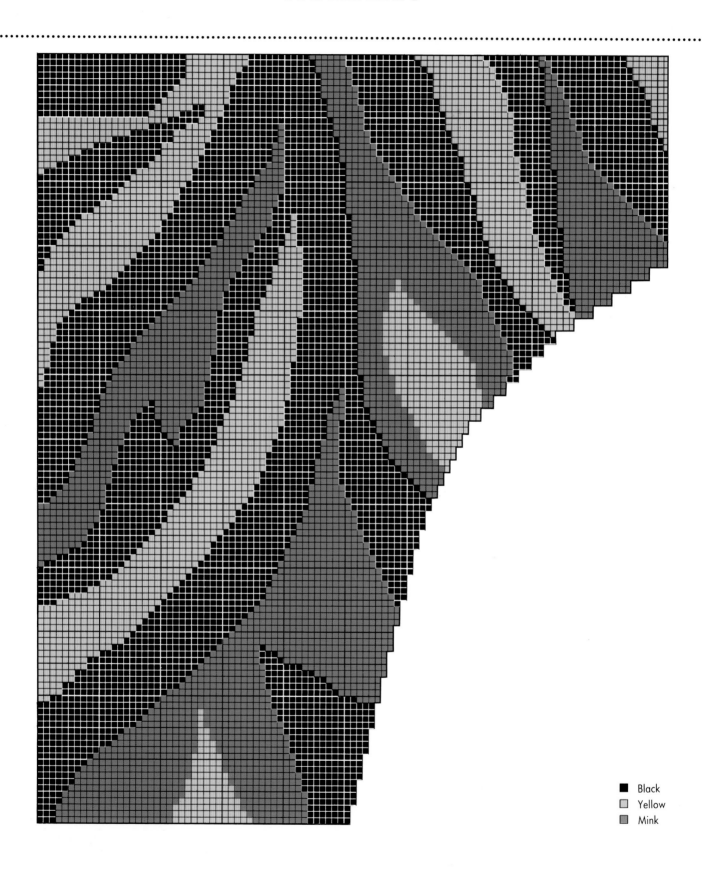

Black
Yellow
Mink

TIGER LILY

worked from start of chart.
Shape neck: cast off 18 sts at beg of next row, then cast off 1 st at neck edge on next 6 rows. Work straight until chart is complete. Leave sts on a spare needle.

RIGHT FRONT

Work as for left front, reading chart in reverse – i.e., reading chart from right to left, work row 1 in purl – and reverse all shapings.

BACK

Work as for jumper.
With RSs of back and fronts facing, knit shoulder seams together.

CUFFS

Work as for jumper.

BUTTONBAND

Using 4½mm needles and black, cast on 10 sts. Work in garter st until band fits neatly from bottom of body ribs to neck shaping. Mark positions for 9 evenly spaced buttons, the first one 8 rows from the hem and the last one 4 rows down from the neckband.

BUTTONHOLE BAND

Using 4½mm needles and black, cast on 10 sts. Work in garter st, making buttonholes to correspond with the pins as follows:
Row 1: k4, cast off 2 sts, k4.
Row 2: k4, cast on 2 sts, k4.
Work straight until buttonhole band fits neatly to neck edge. Cast off.

COLLAR

Using 4½mm needles and black, pick up and knit 10 sts across buttonband, 18 sts up left front, 48 sts across centre back, 18 sts down right front and 10 sts across buttonhole band (104 sts). Work in k1, p1, rib for 2 rows.
Next row: rib 4, cast off 2, rib to end. Return row: rib 98, cast on 2, rib to end. Cont working in k1, p1, rib until collar measures 16cm (6¾in). Cast off in rib.

MAKING UP

Join side and cuff seams as for jumper. Sew on buttons to correspond with buttonholes.

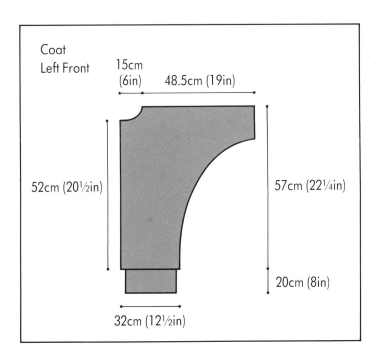

Coat
Left Front
15cm (6in)
48.5cm (19in)
52cm (20½in)
57cm (22¼in)
20cm (8in)
32cm (12½in)

A GIRAFFE CALLED DAISY

A 3-D pink giraffe in a sky of daisies. Work this cheerful, loose-fitting lady's jumper using the intarsia method (see Techniques). The instructions are given for two sizes to fit bust sizes 86/102cm (34/40in).

MATERIALS

Wendy Coconut Ice – 500gm blue (967); 200gm white (953); 100gm coral (948). Scrap of black DK wool for eyes and embroidery.

NEEDLES

One pair of 4mm needles and one pair of 5mm needles. Stitch holders.

TENSION

Using 5mm needles and measured over st st, 17 sts and 26 rows = 10cm (4in) square.

BACK

Using 4mm needles and white, cast on 66/70 sts and work in single rib for 7.5cm (3in), inc 21 sts evenly across last row of rib (87/91 sts). Change to blue and 5mm needles and work in st st from the back chart. Work rows 1-70 inclusive but ignoring the neck shaping, then rep rows 1-65 inclusive, ending with WS facing.

Shape back neck: keeping chart correct, work 32/34 sts, leave remaining sts on a spare needle and work on this first set of sts only. Next row (neck edge, beg of row): cast off 3 sts, work pattern to end. Next row: work from chart. Rep these 2 rows 3 times more (20/22 sts). Work 1 row to end at side edge.

Shape shoulder: cast of all sts. Slip centre 23 sts on to a holder for neckband, rejoin yarn to remaining sts and, keeping chart correct, work to match first side.

FRONT

Using 4mm needles and white, cast on 66/70 sts and work in single rib for 7.5cm (3in), inc 21 sts evenly across last row (87/91 sts). Change to 5mm needles and, working in st st, begin following chart for front until row 131 is complete.

Shape front neck. Next row: work 40/42 sts, leave remaining sts on a spare needle and work on this first set of sts only.

Next row: cast off 4 sts, work chart to end. Next row: work 1 row from chart. Rep these 2 rows once more. Next row: cast off 3 sts, work chart to end. Next row: work 1 row from chart. Rep these last 2 rows 3 times more (20/22 sts). **Shape shoulder**: cast off all sts.

Slip centre 7 sts on to a holder for neckband, rejoin yarn to remaining sts and, keeping chart correct, work to match first side.

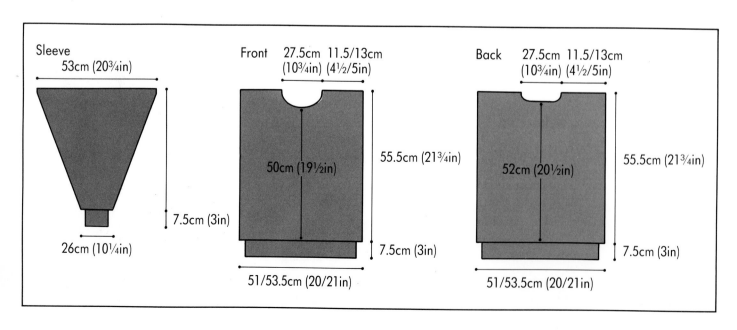

Sleeve
53cm (20¾in)

26cm (10¼in)

7.5cm (3in)

Front   27.5cm   11.5/13cm
        (10¾in) (4½/5in)

50cm (19½in)

55.5cm (21¾in)

7.5cm (3in)

51/53.5cm (20/21in)

Back   27.5cm   11.5/13cm
       (10¾in) (4½/5in)

52cm (20½in)

55.5cm (21¾in)

7.5cm (3in)

51/53.5cm (20/21in)

A GIRAFFE CALLED DAISY

'A Giraffe called Daisy'
Pink 3-D giraffe in a field of
daisies on lady's jumper.

SLEEVES

(Both alike) Using 4mm needles and white, cast on 38 sts and work in k1, p1 rib for 7.5cm (3in), inc 6 sts evenly across last row of rib (44 sts).

Change to 5mm needles and blue and, working in st st, inc 1 st at each end of every 4th row, setting daisy charts as follows:

Work 6 rows in st st (46 sts). Next row: k4 in blue, work 18 sts from daisy chart, k24 in blue. With sts thus set and keeping increases correct, work 16 rows from chart, then work 6 rows in st st in blue (58 sts). Next row: p4 in blue, work 18 sts from daisy chart, p36 in blue. With sts thus set and keeping increases correct, work 16 rows from chart, then 5 rows in st st in blue (68 sts).

Next row: k21 in blue, work 18 sts from chart, work 29 sts in blue. With sts thus set and keeping increases correct, work 16 rows from chart, then 7 rows in st st in blue (80 sts). Next row: k5 in blue, work 18 sts from daisy chart, 57 in blue. With sts thus set and keeping increases correct, work 3 rows from chart (82 sts). Next row: p6 in blue, work 18 sts from chart. With sts thus set and keeping increases and both charts correct, work until both charts have been completed (90 sts). Work 3 rows in st st in blue. Cast off all sts.

NECKBAND

Join right shoulder seam. Using 4mm needles, white and with RS facing, pick up and knit approximately 27 sts down left front neck, 7 sts across centre front, approximately 27 sts up right front neck, approximately 16 sts down right back neck, 23 sts across centre back neck and approximately 16 sts up left back neck. Work in k1, p1 rib for 6.5cm (2½in). Cast off loosely in rib.

EARS

(Make two) Using 5mm needles and coral doubled, cast on 8 sts and work in st st for 4

A GIRAFFE CALLED DAISY

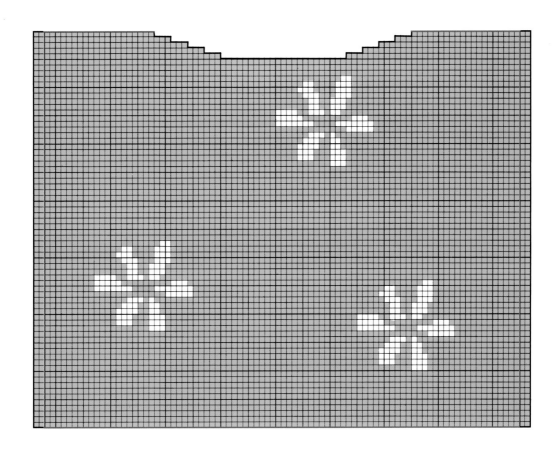

- □ Blue
- □ White
- □ Coral

rows. Dec 1 st at each end of next row, purl 1 row, dec 1 st at each end of next row, purl 1 row. K2, k2 tog, p2 tog, fasten off.

EYEBALLS
(Make two) Using 4mm needles and black DK wool, cast on 3 sts. Knit twice into every st and work in st st for 4 rows. K2 tog 3 times, sl 1, p2 tog, psso. Fasten off. Tie the two ends of yarn together to form a ball.

EYELIDS
(Make two) Using 5mm needles and coral doubled, cast on 6 sts and work in st st for 3 rows. Dec 1 st at each end of next row, cast off. Thread ends back through to cast-on

edge to form eyelashes. Trim.

HORNS
(Make two) Using 5mm needles and white doubled, cast on 10 sts and work in st st for 3 rows. Cast off. Fold in half lengthwise and stitch the two side edges RSs together.

MAKING UP
Using the photograph as a guide, stitch ears on to head along lower edge and catch with one stitch half-way up. Embroider the nose (in satin stitch, see Techniques) and the mouth (in backstitch) on to face. Attach eyeballs in position and sew top edges of eyelids over eyeballs. Sew horns in place.

BIRD-WATCHING

A submerged hippo and a lovebird feature on this tweedy jumper worked using the intarsia method (see Techniques). The boxy shape makes it suitable for both men and women, and it will fit chest size 97-107cm (38-42in).

MATERIALS

Melinda Coss Aran Tweed – 450gm red; 250gm brown; 100gm blue; 50gm green. Melinda Coss Aran Wool – 50gm each of dark grey, light grey, wine, rust, black, ecru, mid-blue, gold and lemon.

NEEDLES

One pair of 3¼mm needles and one pair of 4½mm needles. One small 3¼mm circular needle. Stitch holders.

TENSION

Using 4½mm needles and measured over st st, 18 sts and 25 rows = 10cm (4in) square.

BACK

Using 3¼mm needles and brown, cast on 90 sts. Work in single rib for 25 rows, inc 26 sts evenly across last row of rib (116 sts).

Change to 4½mm needles and begin to follow chart in st st until 90 rows have been worked.

Shape armholes: cast off 5 sts at beg of next 2 rows.* Work 58 rows without shaping.

Shape shoulders: cast off 17 sts at beg of next 2 rows. Cast off 18 sts at beg of following 2 rows. Cast off remaining 36 sts.

FRONT

Work as for back to *. Cont straight until 128 rows of the chart for front have been worked.

Shape neck: k47, work on these sts only, leaving remaining sts on a spare needle. Cast off 4 sts at beg of next row, 3 sts at beg of the following alt row, 2 sts at beg of the next 2 alt rows and 1 st at neck edge on the following

7th row (35 sts). Work straight until front matches back to shoulder shaping ending on a WS row. Cast off 17 sts at beg of next row. Work 1 row, cast off remaining 18 sts. With RS facing, rejoin yarn to remaining sts. Cast off centre 12 sts. Work 1 row. Complete shaping as for first side of neck.

SLEEVES

(Both alike) Using 3¼mm needles and brown, cast on 48 sts. Work in single rib for 30 rows, inc 4 sts evenly across last row of rib (52 sts).

Change to 4½mm needles and begin to follow chart for sleeve, working in st st. Keeping chart correct, inc 1 st at each end of every 4th row until you have 92 sts. Work straight until chart is complete, cast off loosely.

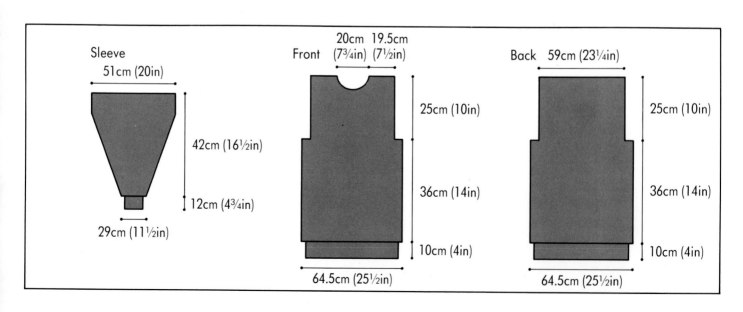

Sleeve
51cm (20in)
42cm (16½in)
12cm (4¾in)
29cm (11½in)

Front
20cm (7¾in) 19.5cm (7½in)
25cm (10in)
36cm (14in)
10cm (4in)
64.5cm (25½in)

Back 59cm (23¼in)
25cm (10in)
36cm (14in)
10cm (4in)
64.5cm (25½in)

BIRD-WATCHING

COLLAR

Join right and left shoulder seams using a flat seam. With RS facing and using a 3¼mm circular needle and brown, knit 32 sts down left side of neck, 12 sts from centre front, 32 sts from right side of neck and 36 sts across back of neck (112 sts). Work in k1, p1 rib for 4 rows, ending at centre front.

Make collar opening: turn, rib back to centre front, turn, rib back to centre front. Cont working in this way for a further 20 rows. Cast off in rib.

MAKING UP

Join sleeves to body. Join side and sleeve seams using a flat seam.

'Bird-watching'
His or hers tweed jumper with submerged hippo and lovebird.

Red
Brown
Blue
Green
Dark grey
Light grey

Wine
Rust
Ecru
Mid-blue
Gold
Lemon
Black

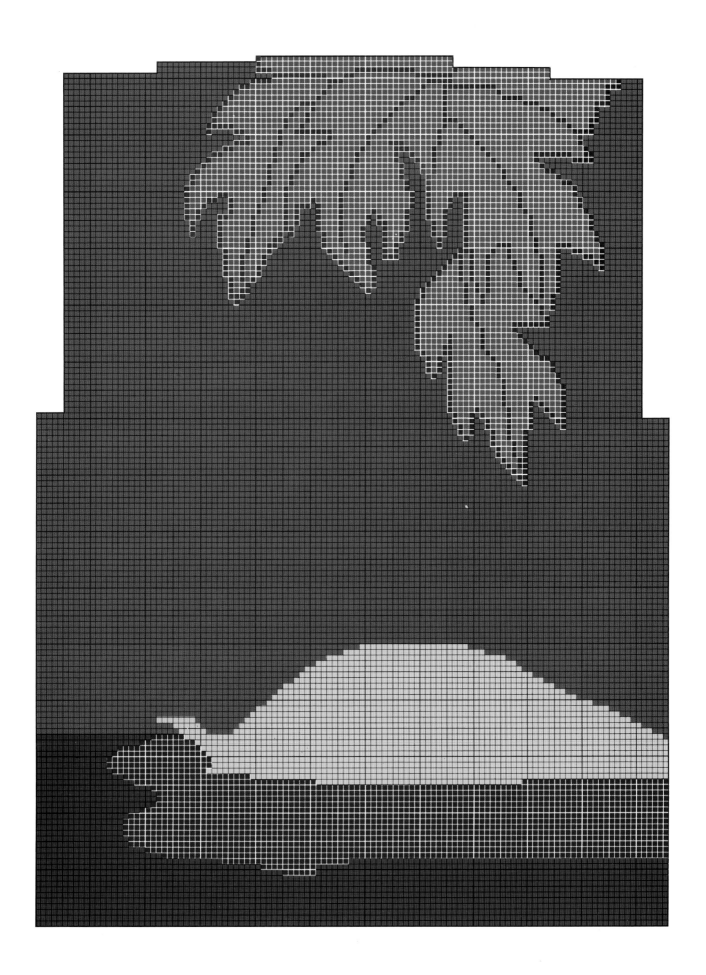

BIRD-WATCHING

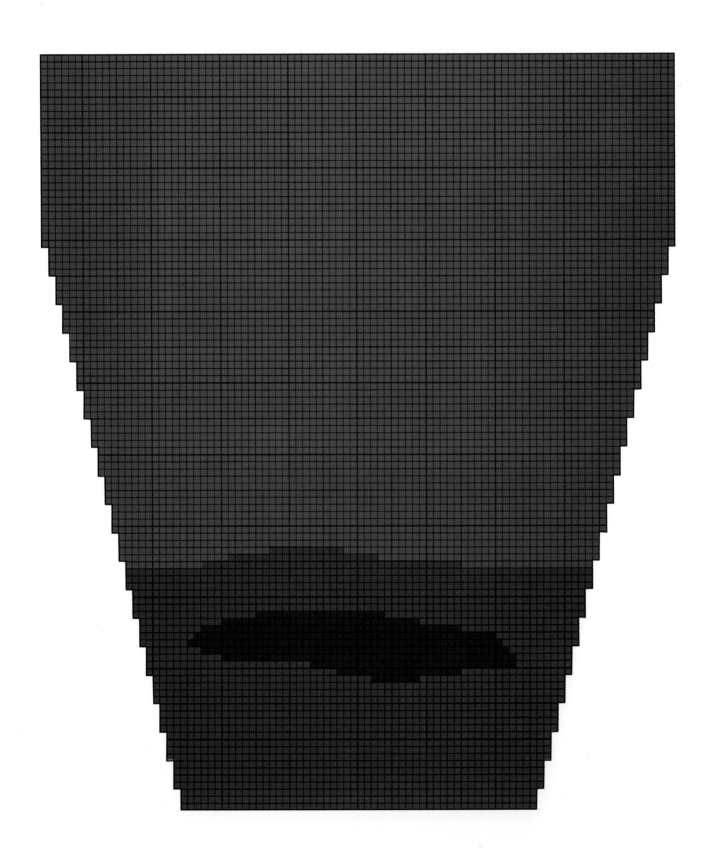

CULTURE VULTURE

While our vulture learns to cook, you can knit this crew-neck jumper in double-knitting wool using the intarsia method (see Techniques). It will fit chest size 97-102cm (38-40in).

FRONT

Using 3¼mm needles and burnt orange, cast on 126 sts and work in single rib for 7.5cm (3in), inc 4 sts evenly across last row of rib (130 sts).

Change to 4mm needles and begin following chart, working in st st to neck shaping. Next row: k54. Leave remaining sts on a spare needle and, working on this first set of sts only, dec 1 st at neck edge on the next 12 rows. Work without further shaping until the chart is complete, cast off remaining 42 sts. Return to sts held on spare needle, slip the centre 22 sts on to a holder and knit to end. Shape neck to match other side. Work straight until chart is complete and cast off remaining 42 sts.

MATERIALS

Standard DK – 300gm burnt orange; 250gm camel; less than 50gm each of brown, black, yellow, white, cream, green, blue and pink.

NEEDLES

One pair of 3¼mm needles and one pair of 4mm needles. Stitch holders.

TENSION

Using 4mm needles and measured over st st, 24 sts and 32 rows = 10cm (4in) square.

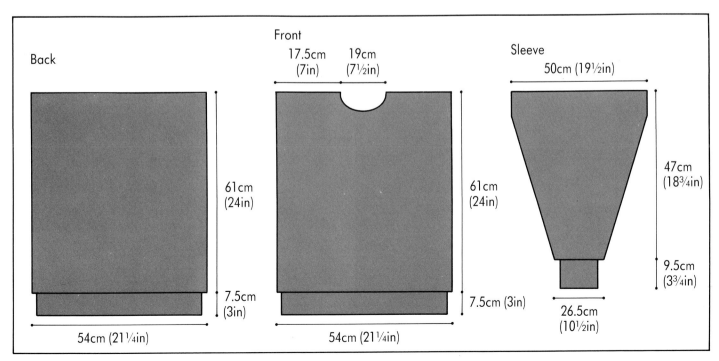

Back — 61cm (24in), 7.5cm (3in), 54cm (21¼in)

Front — 17.5cm (7in), 19cm (7½in), 61cm (24in), 7.5cm (3in), 54cm (21¼in)

Sleeve — 50cm (19½in), 47cm (18¾in), 9.5cm (3¾in), 26.5cm (10½in)

CULTURE VULTURE

BACK

Work as for front but ignore neck shaping and follow chart for back. When chart is complete, **shape shoulders**: cast off 42 sts. Slip centre 46 sts on to a holder and cast off remaining 42 sts.

SLEEVES

(Both alike) Using 3¼mm needles and burnt orange, cast on 50 sts. Work in single rib for 9.5cm (3¾in), inc 14 sts evenly across last row of rib (64 sts). Begin following the sleeve chart. Working in st st, inc 1 st at each end of the 3rd and every following 4th row until you have 118 sts, then inc 1 st at each end of the following 6th row. Work without further shaping until chart is complete. Cast off loosely. Join right shoulder seam.

NECKBAND

Using 3¼mm needles and camel, pick up and knit 21 sts down left side of neck, 22 sts held for centre front neck, 21 sts up right side of neck and 46 sts across centre back (110 sts). Work in single rib for 10cm (4in). Cast off loosely.

MAKING UP

Join left shoulder seam. Join neckband seam and turn inwards. Slip stitch cast-off edge to pick-up edge. Sew sleeves to body and join sleeve and side seams. Use backstitch to sew the word 'recipes' on the book cover as indicated on the front chart.

▨ Burnt orange	□ White		
▨ Camel	□ Cream		
▓ Brown	▨ Green		
■ Black	▨ Blue		
□ Yellow	▨ Pink		

Double-knitting crew-neck jumper for him or her.

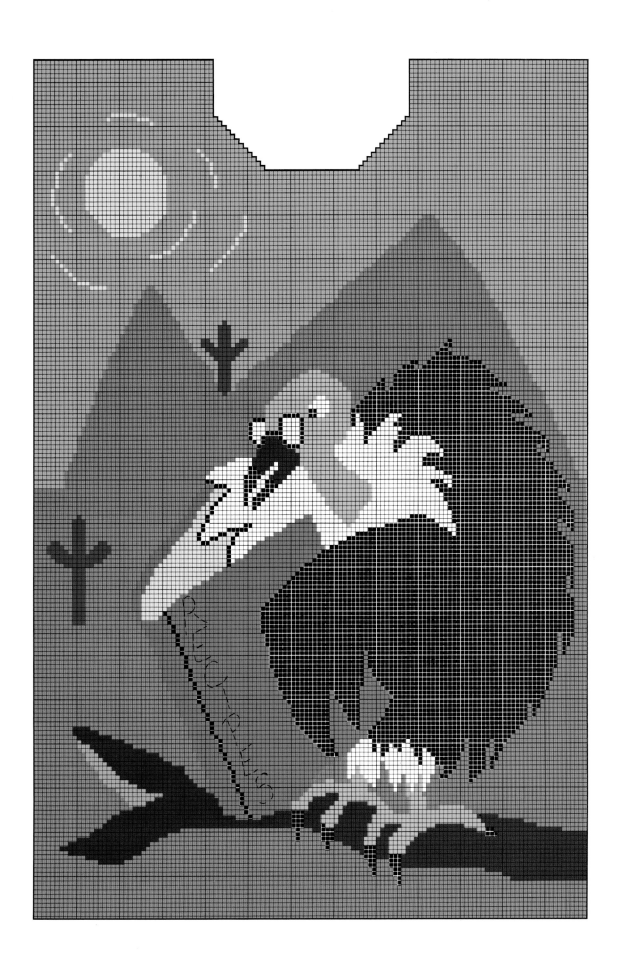

CULTURE VULTURE

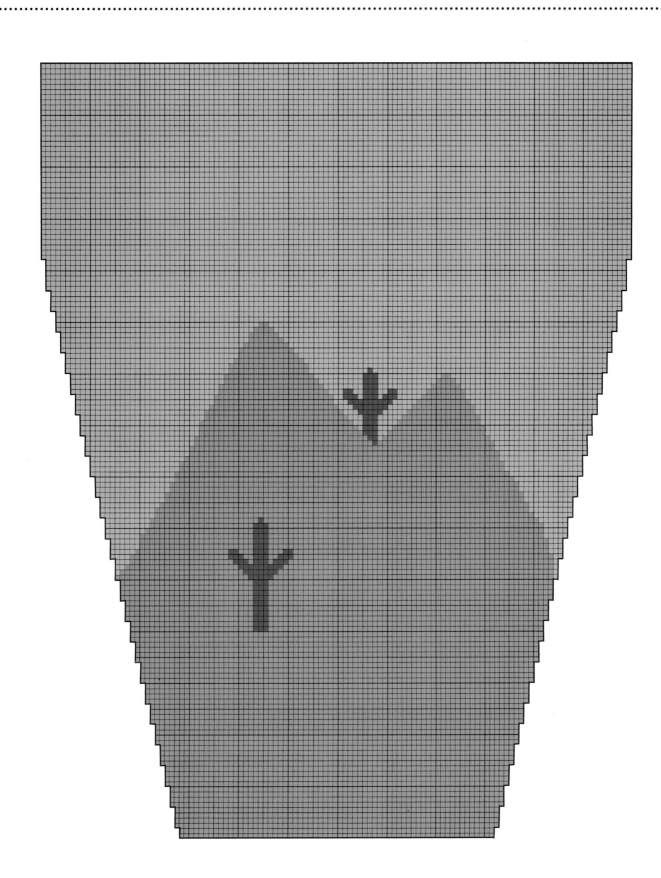

LEGGY BIRD

This bright, double-knit cotton mix sweater is worked using the intarsia method (see Techniques). It will fit up to chest size 107cm (42in).

MATERIALS

Wendy Miami or Standard DK cotton – 450gm white; 50gm each of salmon, grey, jade, green, charcoal, pale blue, turquoise, violet, red, yellow and pink.

NEEDLES

One pair of 3¼mm needles and one pair of 3¾mm needles. Stitch holders.

TENSION

Using 3¾mm needles and measured over st st, 20 sts and 28 rows = 10cm (4in) square.

BACK

Using 3¼mm needles and white, cast on 98 sts and work in k2, p2 rib for 7.5cm (3in), inc 20 sts evenly across last row of rib (118 sts).
Change to 3¾mm needles and work from chart in st st until row 183 is complete.
Shape neck: keeping chart correct, work 46 sts and turn. Work on these sts for first side. Dec 1 st at neck edge on next 6 rows, cont straight until row 190 is complete. Cast off remaining 40 sts. Slip centre 26 sts on to a holder for neckband. Rejoin yarn to remaining sts and, keeping chart correct, shape to match other side of neck. Work straight until chart is complete. Cast off remaining 40 sts.

FRONT

Work as for back, following chart for front until row 173 is complete. **Shape neck**: keeping chart correct, work 48 sts, turn and work on these sts for first side. Dec 1 st at neck edge on every row until 40 sts remain, then cont until row 190 from chart has been worked. Cast off remaining 40 sts. Slip centre 22 sts on to a holder for neckband, rejoin yarn to remaining sts and, keeping chart pattern correct, shape to match other side. When chart is complete, cast off remaining 40 sts.

SLEEVES

(Both alike) Using 3¼mm needles and white, cast on 48 sts and work in k2, p2 rib for 7.5cm (3in), inc 10 sts evenly across last row (58 sts). Change to 3¾mm needles and work from sleeve chart, inc 1 st at each end of every 5th

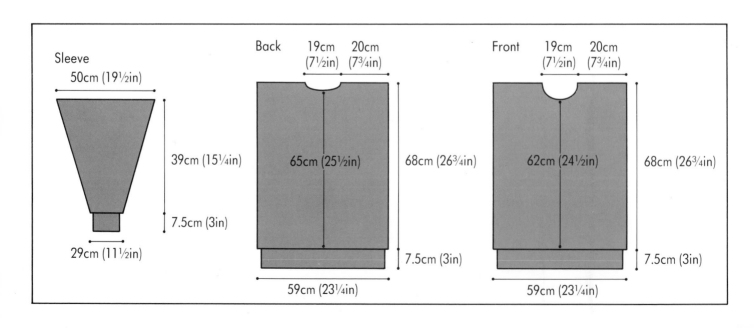

Sleeve
50cm (19½in)
39cm (15¼in)
7.5cm (3in)
29cm (11½in)

Back
19cm (7½in) 20cm (7¾in)
65cm (25½in)
68cm (26¾in)
7.5cm (3in)
59cm (23¼in)

Front
19cm (7½in) 20cm (7¾in)
62cm (24½in)
68cm (26¾in)
7.5cm (3in)
59cm (23¼in)

row until you have 100 sts. Complete chart, cast off loosely.
Join left shoulder seam.

NECKBAND
Using 3¼mm needles, white and with RS facing, pick up and knit 15 sts down left front neck, 22 sts across centre front, 15 sts up right front neck, 7 sts down right back neck, 26 sts across centre back, 7 sts up left back neck (92 sts). Work in k2, p2 rib for 6 rows. Cast off in rib.

MAKING UP
Join right shoulder and neckband seams. Sew on sleeves and join sleeve and side seams. Join neck rib using a flat seam.

'Leggy Bird'
Lady's summer jumper in bright cotton.

White
Salmon
Grey
Jade
Green
Charcoal
Pale blue
Turquoise
Violet
Red
Yellow
Pink

LEGGY BIRD

G'DAY SUNSHINE

This koala bear jumper is knitted in a chunky alpaca mix yarn, with instructions given for two sizes to fit 97/126cm (38/46in). It is worked using the intarsia method (see Techniques).

FRONT

Using 5½mm needles and ecru, cast on 59/67 sts. Work in k1, p1 rib for 8cm (3¼in), inc 21/21 sts evenly across last row of rib (80/88 sts).*

Change to 6½mm needles. Begin following chart in st st, working to neck shaping.

Next row: work 34/38 sts, leave remaining sts on a spare needle. Working on this first set of sts only, turn, work 1 row, dec 1 st at neck edge on the next 6 rows. Work until chart is complete, cast off remaining 28/32 sts. Return to remaining sts and, with RS facing, slip centre 12 sts on to a stitch holder, knit to end of row, then shape neck as for other side.

BACK

Work as for front to *.

Change to 6½mm needles and cont as follows:

k20/24, work 39 sts from chart, k to end. Next row: p21/25, work 39 sts from sleeve chart, p to end. Work as set until chart is complete, then cont straight in beige only, omitting neck shaping until back matches front to shoulder. Cast off 28/32 sts, work centre 24 sts, cast off remaining 28/32 sts. Slip centre 24 sts on to a holder.

RIGHT SLEEVE

Using 5½mm needles and ecru, cast on 29/31 sts. Work in k1, p1 rib for 8cm (3¼in), inc 11/11 sts evenly across last row of rib (40/42 sts).

Change to 6½mm needles and beige. Next row: k1/2, knit first row from sleeve chart, k1/2. Cont working in st st with chart in this position for 60 rows. **At the same time**, inc 1 st at each end of 3rd row and every following alt row until you have 64/68 sts,

MATERIALS
Wendy Orinoco Chunky – 350/400gm beige; 350gm ecru; 100gm pale grey; and 50gm each of brown and dark grey.

NEEDLES
One pair of 5½mm needles and one pair of 6½mm needles. Stitch holders.

TENSION
Using 6½mm needles and measured over st st, 14 sts and 20 rows = 10cm (4in) square.

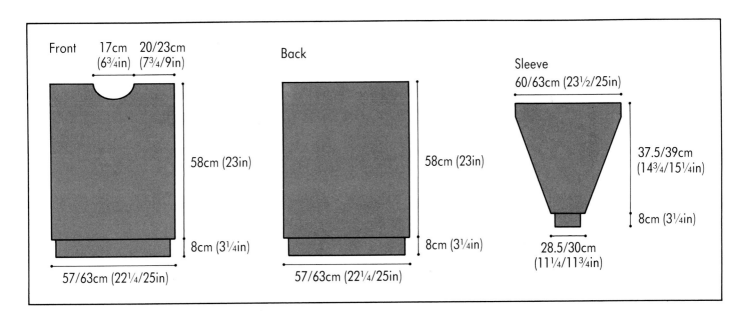

Front 17cm (6¾in) 20/23cm (7¾/9in)
58cm (23in)
8cm (3¼in)
57/63cm (22¼/25in)

Back
58cm (23in)
8cm (3¼in)
57/63cm (22¼/25in)

Sleeve
60/63cm (23½/25in)
37.5/39cm (14¾/15¼in)
8cm (3¼in)
28.5/30cm (11¼/11¾in)

G'DAY SUNSHINE

'G'day Sunshine'
Chunky alpaca lady's jumper in neutral colours.

then on every following 4th row until you have 84/88 sts. When chart is complete, cont in base colour only. When shapings are complete, cont straight until work measures 45.5/47cm (18/18½in).

LEFT SLEEVE
Work as for right sleeve but work rib in beige and background in ecru. Join right shoulder seam.

NECKBAND
Using 5½mm needles, ecru and with RS facing, pick up and knit 15 sts down left front neck, 12 sts from front neck stitch holder, 15 sts up right front neck and 24 sts from back neck stitch holder (66 sts). Work in k1, p1 rib for 6.5cm (2½in). Cast off loosely in rib.

MAKING UP
Join left shoulder seam and join neckband. Fold neckband inwards and slip stitch cast-off edge to pick-up edge. Using a flat seam, join sleeves to jumper, and join side and sleeve seams.

☐ Beige
☐ Ecru
☐ Pale grey
▨ Brown
■ Dark grey

G'DAY SUNSHINE

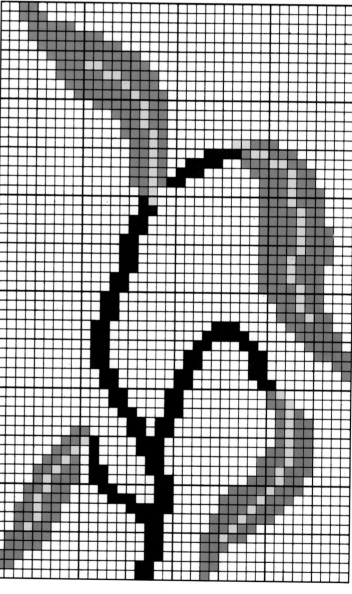

HANGING AROUND

This cheeky chimpanzee crew-neck jumper for children is worked in double-knitting wool using the intarsia method (see Techniques). Simple to knit and fun to wear, the instructions are given in two sizes to fit chest sizes up to 66/71cm (26/28in).

FRONT

Using 3¼mm needles and black, cast on 84/88 sts. Work in k2, p2 rib until work measures 5cm (2in), inc 1/3 sts evenly across last row of rib (85/91 sts).

Change to 4mm needles and begin following chart in st st for 100/112 rows. **Shape neck**. Next row (RS): k34/37, leave remaining sts on a spare needle and, working on the first set of sts only, dec 1 st at neck edge on the next 2 rows and the following 6/6 alt rows (26/29 sts). Work straight for 4/4 rows and cast off remaining sts. Return to work held on spare needle and slip centre 17/17 sts on to a holder, rejoin yarn to remaining sts and shape to match first side.

BACK

Using 3¼mm needles and base colour, cast

MATERIALS

Standard DK – 200gm blue; 150gm black; less than 50gm each of brown, white, yellow, lemon, chestnut and beige.

NEEDLES

One pair of 3¼mm needles and one pair of 4mm needles. Stitch holders.

TENSION

Using 4mm needles and measured over st st, 24 sts and 32 rows = 10cm (4in) square.

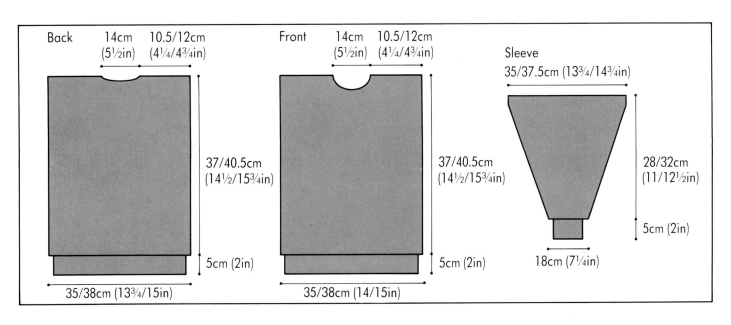

Back   14cm (5½in)   10.5/12cm (4¼/4¾in)   37/40.5cm (14½/15¾in)   5cm (2in)   35/38cm (13¾/15in)

Front   14cm (5½in)   10.5/12cm (4¼/4¾in)   37/40.5cm (14½/15¾in)   5cm (2in)   35/38cm (14/15in)

Sleeve   35/37.5cm (13¾/14¾in)   28/32cm (11/12½in)   5cm (2in)   18cm (7¼in)

HANGING AROUND

on 84/88 sts. Work in k2, p2 rib until work measures 5cm (2in), inc 1/3 sts evenly across last row of rib (85/91 sts).

Change to 4mm needles and begin following chart for back, working in st st for 116/128 rows. **Shape neck**. Next row: work 27/30 sts, turn, dec 1 st at beg of next row, work to end and cast off remaining 26/29 sts. Slip centre 31/31 sts on to a holder, rejoin yarn to remaining sts and shape to match other side.

SLEEVES

(Both alike) Using 3¼mm needles and base colour, cast on 44/44 sts. Work 5cm (2in) in k2, p2 rib ending with a WS row.

Change to 4mm needles and work in st st, inc 1 st at each end of the next and every following alt row until you have 50/50 sts, then on every following 4th row until you have 84/90 sts. Cont without further shaping until sleeve measures 33/37 cm (13/14½in), ending with a WS row. Cast off loosely. Join left shoulder seam.

NECKBAND

Using 3¼mm needles, base colour and with RS facing, pick up and knit 31/31 sts from back stitch holder, 17/19 sts down left side neck, 17/17 sts held for front and 17/19 sts up right side neck (82/86 sts). Work 8 rows in k2, p2 rib, knit 1 row. Work 8 more rows in k2, p2 rib. Cast off loosely.

MAKING UP

Join right shoulder seam. Fold neckband inwards and slip stitch cast-off edge to pick-up edge. Join sleeves to jumper and join side and sleeve seams.

■ Blue
■ Black
■ Brown
□ White
□ Yellow
□ Lemon
□ Beige
■ Chestnut

'Hanging Around'
Kids crew-neck jumper with chimp eating banana.

SNAPPY DRESSER

The crocodile on this Aran-weight children's sweater is in danger of snapping off his own tail! Worked in stocking stitch using the intarsia method (see Techniques), it is quoted in four sizes to fit chest sizes 66/71/76/86cm (26/28/30/34in).

FRONT

Using 3¾mm needles and ecru, cast on 63/67/71/77 sts and work in single rib for 2 rows. Change to red, cont in single rib for 18 more rows, inc 7/9/11/11 sts evenly across last row of rib (70/76/82/88 sts).

Change to 4½mm needles and begin following chart, working in st st. When chart is complete, work straight in base colour only until work measures 33/35/39/42cm (13/13¾/15¼/16½in), ending with a WS row. **Shape neck**: k19/22/25/28. Slip these sts on to a spare needle, cast off centre 32 sts, knit to end. Cont until work measures 48/51/54/57cm (19/20/21¼/22¼in) from start. Cast off. Return to sts held for other side of neck and work to match first side.

BACK

Work as for front, following chart for back and ignoring neck shaping. When chart is complete, work straight in base colour only until back matches front to shoulder, Cast off all sts.

SLEEVES

(Both alike) Using 3¾mm needles and ecru, cast on 33/33/33/35 sts and work in single rib for 2 rows. Change to red and cont in rib until work measures 5/5/6.5/6.5cm (2/2/2½/2½in), inc 6/10/10/8 sts evenly across last row of rib (39/43/43/43 sts).

Change to 4½mm needles and work in st st, inc 1 st at each end of the 5th and every following 6th/6th/4th/4th row until you have 51/51/55/67 sts. Last three sizes only: inc 1 st at each end of every following 8th/6th/6th row until you have 55/65/71 sts. All sizes: cont by inc 1 st at each end of every 6th/8th/6th/6th row until you have 57/61/71/77 sts.

MATERIALS

Standard Aran – 300/350/350/400gm red; 50gm each of green, brown, black, ecru and stone.

NEEDLES

One pair of 3¾mm needles and one pair of 4½mm needles. Stitch holders.

TENSION

Using 4½mm needles and measured over st st, 19 sts and 24 rows = 10cm (4in) square.

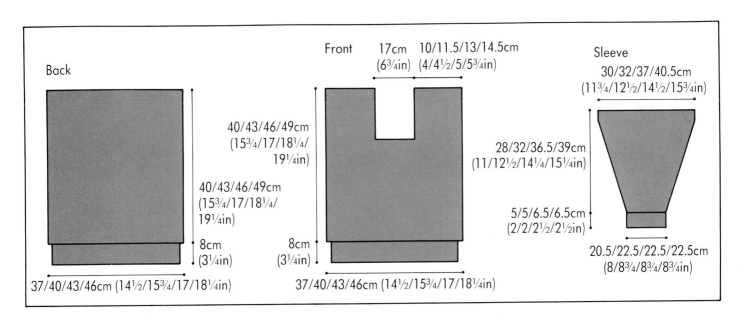

Back

Front — 17cm (6¾in) — 10/11.5/13/14.5cm (4/4½/5/5¾in)

Sleeve — 30/32/37/40.5cm (11¾/12½/14½/15¾in)

40/43/46/49cm (15¾/17/18¼/19¼in)

40/43/46/49cm (15¾/17/18¼/19¼in)

8cm (3¼in)

8cm (3¼in)

28/32/36.5/39cm (11/12½/14¼/15¼in)

5/5/6.5/6.5cm (2/2/2½/2½in)

37/40/43/46cm (14½/15¾/17/18¼in)

37/40/43/46cm (14½/15¾/17/18¼in)

20.5/22.5/22.5/22.5cm (8/8¾/8¾/8¾in)

SNAPPY DRESSER

Cont without further shaping until sleeve measures 33/37/43/45.5cm (13/14½/17/18in) from start. Cast off loosely.
Join shoulder seams.

COLLAR
Using 3¾mm needles and base colour, cast on 94 sts. Work in single rib until work measures 17cm (6¾in). Change to ecru, rib 1 row. Cast off in ecru.

MAKING UP
Join sleeves to jumper and join side and sleeve seams. Stitch short end of neckband to bottom neck opening on front. Stitch cast-on edge of neckband up right front neck, across back, down left front neck and across front. Fold back.
NB Collar should cross right over left for girls and left over right for boys.

■ Red
■ Green
■ Brown
■ Black
□ Ecru
■ Stone

'Snappy Dresser'
Kids Aran-weight crew-neck with croc
snapping his own tail.

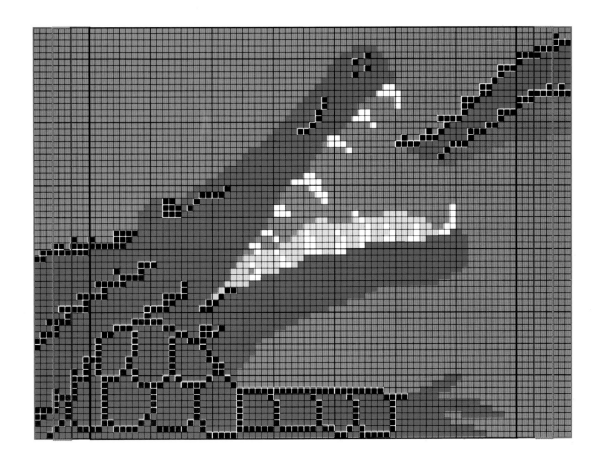

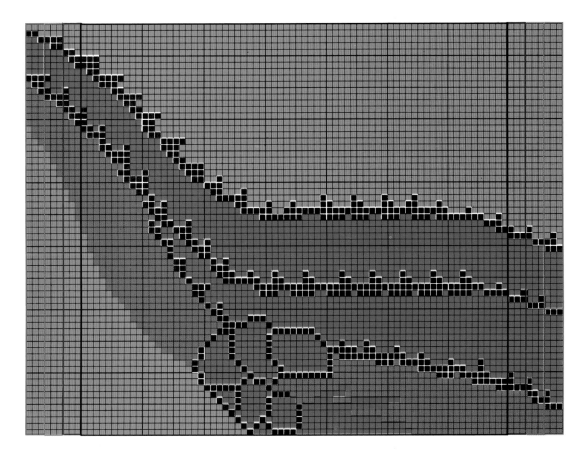

TURN TURTLE

This cropped, shirt-style jumper is knitted in Aran-weight yarn using the intarsia method (see Techniques) and will fit chest size 92-102cm (36-40in). It should take you less time to knit than it has taken our turtle to walk around the jumper.

MATERIALS
Standard Aran – 200gm white; 100gm each of jade, red and royal blue; 50gm each of mid-blue, light brown and stone. 3 buttons, 15mm (³⁄₄mm) in diameter.

NEEDLES
One pair of 3¾mm needles, one pair of 4mm needles and one pair of 4½mm needles; one short circular 3¾mm needle. Stitch holders.

TENSION
Using 4½mm needles and measured over st st, 19 sts and 24 rows = 10cm (4in) square.

BACK
Using 3¾mm needles and white, cast on 100 sts. Work in k1, p1 rib for 26 rows, inc 6 sts evenly across last row of rib (106 sts).
Change to 4½mm needles and begin working from chart in st st. Work without shaping until chart is complete.
Place 38 sts on stitch holders for each shoulder and 30 sts for centre back neck.

FRONT
Work as for back until 84 rows of the chart have been completed. Divide for neck. Next row: work 49 sts, turn, cont working on these 49 sts for 23 rows, then dec 1 st at neck edge on next 11 rows. Work 2 rows. Leave remaining 38 sts on a holder. Return to sts held for other side. Slip centre 8 sts on to a safety-pin. Join yarn to remaining 49 sts and work to match first side.

SLEEVES
(Both alike) Using 3¾mm needles and white, cast on 37 sts. Work in k1, p1 rib for 20 rows, inc 31 sts evenly across last row of rib (68 sts). Change to 4½mm needles and jade and work 30 rows from sleeve chart, repeating the fence motif across the row. When 30 rows have been completed, change to red and cont following chart as before. When 30 rows have been completed, change to royal blue and work 30 rows in this colourway. **At the same time** inc 1 st at each end of every 6th row until you have 96 sts. When third repeat of sleeve chart is completed, cast off.

BUTTONBAND
Using 3¾mm needles and white, pick up 8 sts from safety-pin and work in k1, p1 rib until band reaches top of the neck opening when slightly stretched. Cast off in rib. With pins,

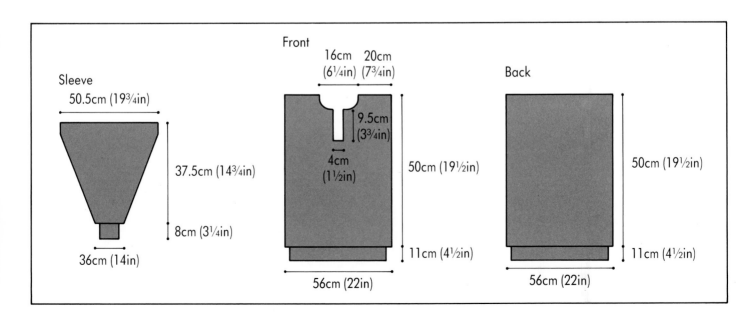

Sleeve
50.5cm (19¾in)

37.5cm (14¾in)

8cm (3¼in)

36cm (14in)

Front
16cm   20cm
(6¼in)   (7¾in)

9.5cm (3¾in)

4cm (1½in)

50cm (19½in)

11cm (4½in)

56cm (22in)

Back

50cm (19½in)

11cm (4½in)

56cm (22in)

TURN TURTLE

mark positions for three buttons evenly up the band.

BUTTONHOLE BAND

Using 3¾mm needles and white, pick up 8 sts over those originally held on safety-pin. Work in k1, p1 rib to first button position, then make buttonholes as follows:
Row 1: rib 3, cast off 2, rib 3.
Row 2: rib 3, cast on 2, rib 3.
Cont in rib making buttonholes to correspond with pins. Work straight until band fits neatly to neck edge, cast off in rib.

COLLAR

With wrong sides of back and front facing each other, knit together and cast off shoulder seams in white (seam should be on RS of work, see Techniques).

Using a 3¾mm circular needle, white and with RS facing, pick up and knit 16 sts up right front neck, 30 sts from centre back stitch holder, 16 sts down left front neck. Work 6 rows in k1, p1 rib.

Change to 4mm needles and cont in rib, inc 1 st at each end of the next and every alt row by picking up the loop between the first and second st and knitting into it. Cont working in this way until you have 78 sts. **At the same time** when you have worked 14 rows from the start, change to 4½mm needles. Work straight until collar measures 12cm (4¾in) at centre back. Cast off loosely in rib.

MAKING UP

Join sleeves to jumper. Join side and sleeve seams. Sew on buttonbands (crossing right over left for women and left over right for men). Sew on buttons to correspond with buttonholes.

☐	White
■	Jade
■	Red
■	Royal blue
■	Mid-blue
■	Light brown
☐	Stone

'Turn Turtle'
Cropped Aran-weight lady's
shirt-style jumper.

TURN TURTLE

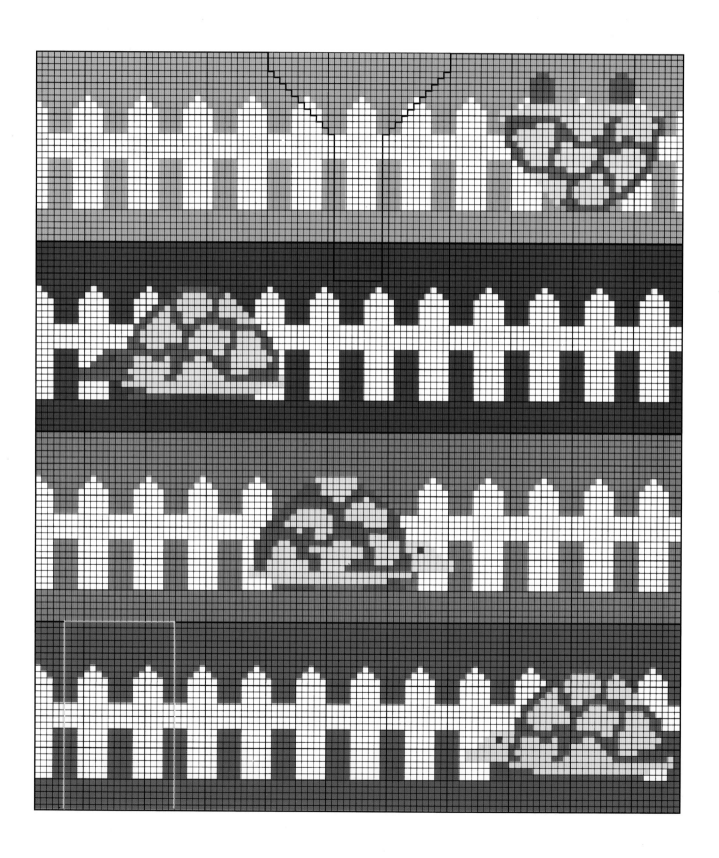

THE MANE ATTRACTION

This slash-neck zebra jumper with a mane is worked in a soft, fluffy double-knitting yarn using the intarsia method (see Techniques). Instructions are given for three sizes to fit chest sizes 92/97/102cm (36/38/40in).

FRONT

Using 3½mm needles and jade, cast on 116/120/128 sts. Work in k2, p2 rib for 6.5cm (2½in), inc 1/3/1 sts in last row of rib (117/123/129 sts).

Change to 4mm needles and work straight in st st for 74 rows.* Next row (RS): begin following chart in st st until it is complete.

Next row (RS): cast off 39/42/45 sts, p39 knit to end.

Next row: cast off 39/42/45 sts, p39. Cont working in st st on this centre set of 39 sts for 2.5cm (1in). Cast off.

BACK

Work as for front to *. Cont following chart but reverse the image – i.e., read chart beginning with a purl row and working knit rows from left to right and purl rows from right to left – as you look at the chart you are seeing the WS of your work. Complete chart, then work neck and shoulder shaping as for front.

RIGHT SLEEVE

Using 3½mm needles and jade, cast on 52/52/56 sts. Work in k2, p2 rib for 6.5cm (2½in), inc 7/11/7 sts evenly across last row of rib (59/63/63 sts).

Change to 4mm needles and begin following chart in st st, inc 1 st at each end of 5th/3rd/3rd row and every following 4th/2nd/2nd row until you have 115/79/79 sts on the needle. 2nd and 3rd sizes only: inc 1st at each end of every following 4th row until you have 127/127 sts on the needle. Complete chart and cast off.

LEFT SLEEVE

Work as for right sleeve but work in plain jade (omitting stripes).

MATERIALS
Standard DK – 300/350/350gm jade; 150gm each of white and black.

NEEDLES
One pair of 3½mm needles and one pair of 4mm needles.

TENSION
Using 4mm needles and measured over st st, 24 sts and 32 rows = 10cm (4in).

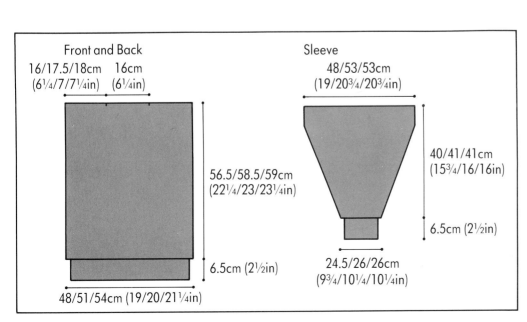

Front and Back
16/17.5/18cm   16cm
(6¼/7/7¼in)   (6¼in)

56.5/58.5/59cm
(22¼/23/23¼in)

6.5cm (2½in)

48/51/54cm (19/20/21¼in)

Sleeve
48/53/53cm
(19/20¾/20¾in)

40/41/41cm
(15¾/16/16in)

6.5cm (2½in)

24.5/26/26cm
(9¾/10¼/10¼in)

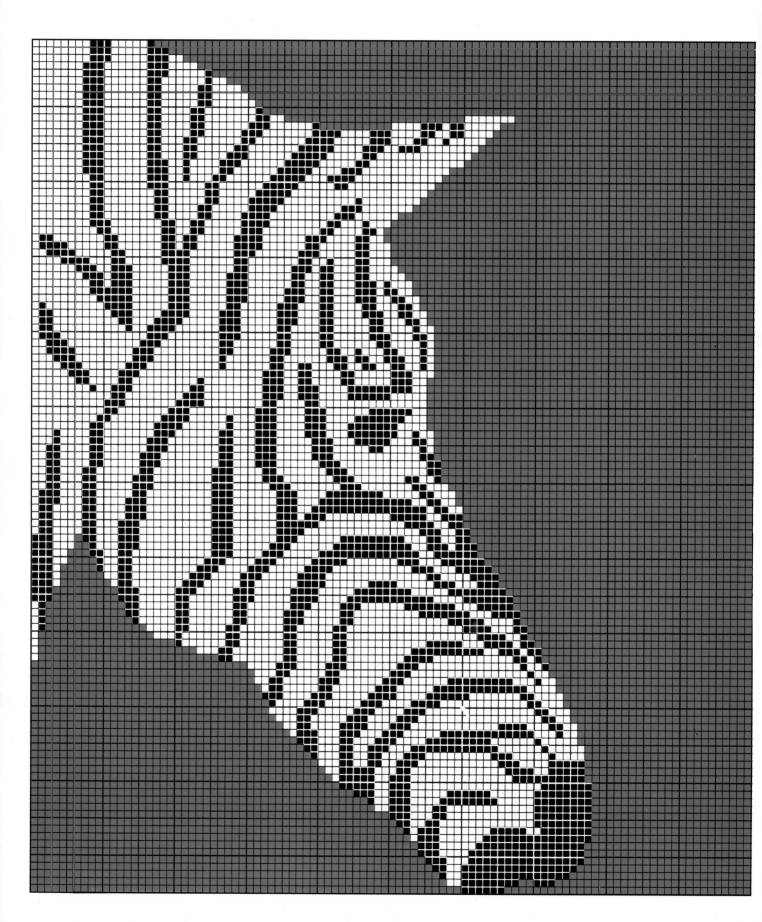

THE MANE ATTRACTION

Jade
White
Black

'The Mane Attraction'
Soft, fluffy zebra jumper with mane.

THE MANE ATTRACTION

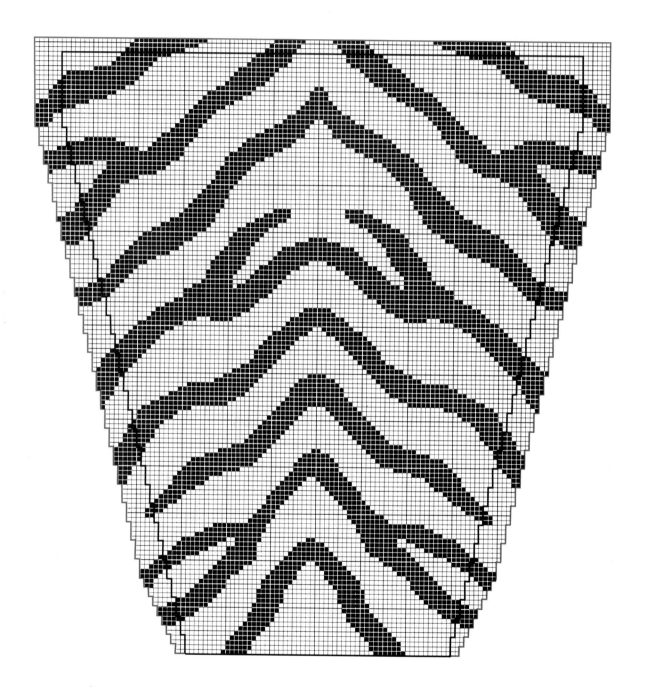

MAKING UP

Fold neckbands in so that RS purl row forms top edge. Catch into place. Fold sleeves in half lengthways and mark centre stitch. Using black and white wool alternately, knot a fringe to form mane, starting at the centre top of the right sleeve and ending half-way down. Join shoulder seams, continue mane across right shoulder to point on graph marked with a red dot. Join sleeves to body. Join side and sleeve seams.

MEAN CAT

This slinky jumper in double-knitting yarn is simple to knit and is worked using the intarsia method (see Techniques). It will fit bust size 92cm (36in).

FRONT

Using 3¼mm needles and black, cast on 110 sts. Work in k1, p1 rib for 20 rows.

Change to 4mm needles and begin following chart in st st, working without shaping for 20 rows. Dec 1 st at each end of next row and every following 4th row until you have 90 sts. Work 12 rows without shaping, then inc 1 st at each end of next row and every following 4th row until you have 110 sts. Work 6 rows straight.

Shape armholes: cast off 4 sts at beg of the next 2 rows, then dec 1 st, at each end of the next 5 rows and the following 2 alt rows until you have 88 sts. Cont straight to neck shaping.

Next row: work 32 sts, leave remaining sts on a spare needle and, working on this first set of sts only, dec 1 st at neck edge on the next 4 rows, then dec 1 st at neck edge on the next 5 alt rows. Work straight until chart is complete, cast off. Return to held sts and slip centre 24 sts on to a stitch holder. Rejoin yarn and shape to match first side.

BACK

Work as for front but reverse shapings by working right to left rows as purl and left to right rows as knit. Work in the diagonal stripe sequence only – i.e., ignore panther – and work straight to back neck shaping.

Next row: work 27 sts, leave remaining sts on a spare needle and, working on this first set of sts only, dec 1 st at neck edge on the next 4 rows. Work straight until chart is complete, cast off remaining 23 sts. Slip centre 34 sts on to a spare needle and rejoin yarn to remaining

MATERIALS

Standard DK – 300gm black; 250gm red; 50gm each of grey and white.

NEEDLES

One pair of 3¼mm needles and one pair of 4mm needles. Stitch holders.

TENSION

Using 4mm needles and measured over st, st, 24 sts and 32 rows = 10cm (4in) square.

'Mean Cat'
Lady's slinky double-knitting wool jumper in red and black.

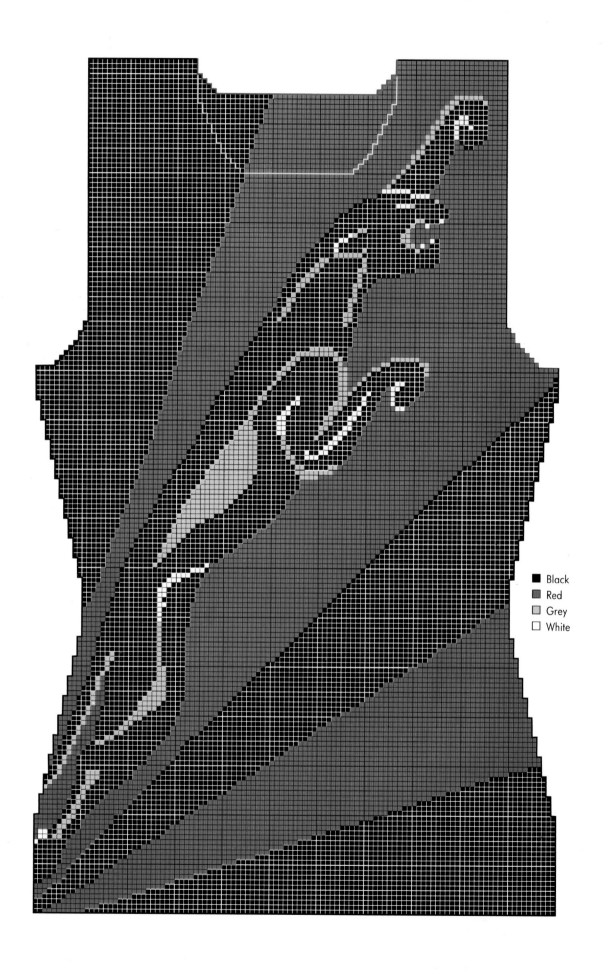

Black
Red
Grey
White

MEAN CAT

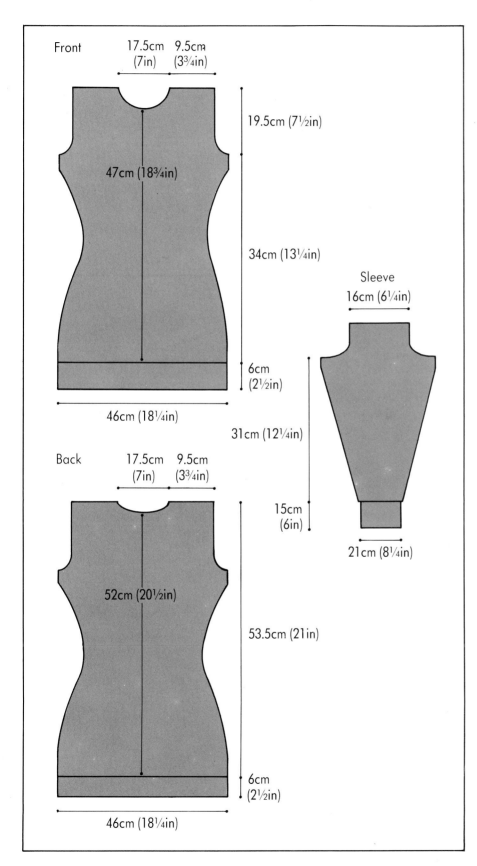

Front

17.5cm (7in)   9.5cm (3¾in)

47cm (18¾in)

19.5cm (7½in)

34cm (13¼in)

6cm (2½in)

46cm (18¼in)

Back

17.5cm (7in)   9.5cm (3¾in)

52cm (20½in)

53.5cm (21in)

6cm (2½in)

46cm (18¼in)

Sleeve

16cm (6¼in)

31cm (12¼in)

15cm (6in)

21cm (8¼in)

sts. Shape to match other side, working until chart is complete. Cast off remaining 23 sts.

RIGHT SLEEVE

Using 3¼mm needles and black, cast on 50 sts. Work in k1, p1 rib until cuff measures 15cm (6in).
Change to 4mm needles and cont in st st, inc 1 st at each end of the next and every following 6th row until you have 80 sts. Cont straight until sleeve measures 46cm (18¼in). **Shape sleeve top**: cast off 4 sts at beg of next 2 rows, then dec 1 st at each end of next 5 rows and the following 4 alt rows. Then dec 1 st at each end of the 8 following 4th rows (38 sts). Work 2 rows straight. Cast off all sts.

LEFT SLEEVE

Work as for right sleeve but use red through-out instead of black.

ROLL NECK

Join left shoulder seam. Using 3¼mm nee-dles and black, pick up and knit 28 sts down left front, 24 sts held for centre front, 28 sts up right front, 4 sts down right back, 34 sts across centre back and 4 sts down left back (122 sts). Work in k1, p1 rib for 9cm (3½in). Change to 4mm needles and work in k1, p1 rib for 9cm (3½in). Cast off loosely.

MAKING UP

Join right shoulder seam. Sew in sleeves, easing fullness at top. Sew up side and sleeve seams. Join neckband.

SEALED WITH A FISH

This summer jumper is knitted in supersoft cotton mix double-knitting yarn. It is worked in stocking stitch using the intarsia method (see Techniques), and anyone who has tackled multi-coloured work before should find it easy to knit. The instructions are given for four sizes, to fit chest sizes 96/102/107/112cm (38/40/42/44in).

MATERIALS

DK cotton – 300gm blue; 150gm turquoise; 100gm grey; less than 50gm each of white, black, salmon, coral and taupe.

NEEDLES

One pair of 3¼mm needles and one pair of 4mm needles. Stitch holders.

TENSION

Using 4mm needles and measured over st st, 22 sts and 31 rows = 10cm (4in) square.

FRONT

Using 3¼mm needles and grey, cast on 95/99/105/111 sts. Work in single rib for 8cm (3¼in), inc 22/24/24/22 sts evenly across last row of rib (117/123/129/133 sts).

Change to 4mm needles and begin following chart in st st until row 162/162/166/166 is complete. **Shape neck:** k47/50/53/55. Slip remaining sts on to a spare needle and, working on the first set of sts only, purl 1 row. Dec 1 st at neck edge on the next row and the 4 following rows. Then dec 1 st at neck edge on every alt row 5/5/6/6 times (37/40/43/44 sts). Work straight until chart is complete and cast off remaining sts.

Slip centre 23/23/23/23 sts on to a stitch

holder. With RS facing, rejoin yarn to remaining sts and knit to end. Shape to match other side of neck.

BACK

Work as for front, following chart for back and ignoring neck shaping instructions. When chart is complete, cast off all sts.

SLEEVES

(Both alike) Using 3¼mm needles and blue, cast on 51/53/55/57 sts. Work in single rib for 7cm (2¾in), inc 14/16/18/22 sts evenly across last row of rib (65/69/73/75 sts).

Change to 4mm needles and begin following chart for sleeve in st st. First three sizes: inc 1

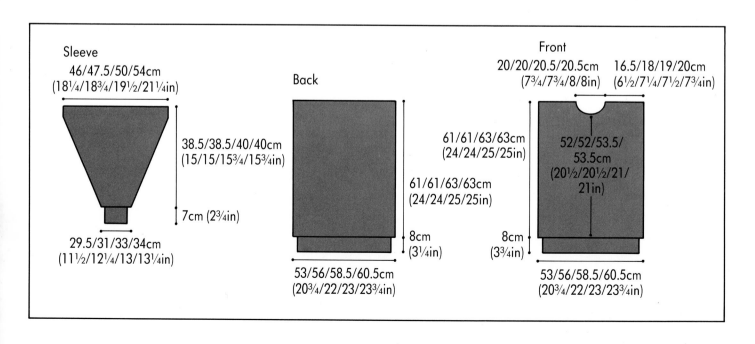

Sleeve
46/47.5/50/54cm
(18¼/18¾/19½/21¼in)

38.5/38.5/40/40cm
(15/15/15¾/15¾in)

7cm (2¾in)

29.5/31/33/34cm
(11½/12¼/13/13¼in)

Back

61/61/63/63cm
(24/24/25/25in)

61/61/63/63cm
(24/24/25/25in)

8cm
(3¼in)

53/56/58.5/60.5cm
(20¾/22/23/23¾in)

Front
20/20/20.5/20.5cm
(7¾/7¾/8/8in)

16.5/18/19/20cm
(6½/7¼/7½/7¾in)

52/52/53.5/53.5cm
(20½/20½/21/21in)

8cm
(3¾in)

53/56/58.5/60.5cm
(20¾/22/23/23¾in)

SEALED WITH A FISH

st at each end of every 6th row until you have 101/105/111 sts. Fourth size only: inc 1 st at each end of the 6th row and every following 5th row until you have 119 sts. All sizes: work without further shaping until the chart is complete. Cast off loosely.
Join left shoulder seam.

NECKBAND
Using 3¼mm needles and blue, pick up and knit 23/23/24/24 sts down left front, 23 sts held for centre front, 23/23/24/24 sts up right front and 43/43/45/45 sts across centre back (112/112/116/116 sts). Work in k1, p1 rib for 10 rows. Cast off.

MAKING UP
Join right shoulder seam. Join neck rib. Sew sleeves to jumper. Join side and sleeve seams.

'Sealed with a Fish'
One-size cotton seal sweatshirt.
Seal at feeding time.

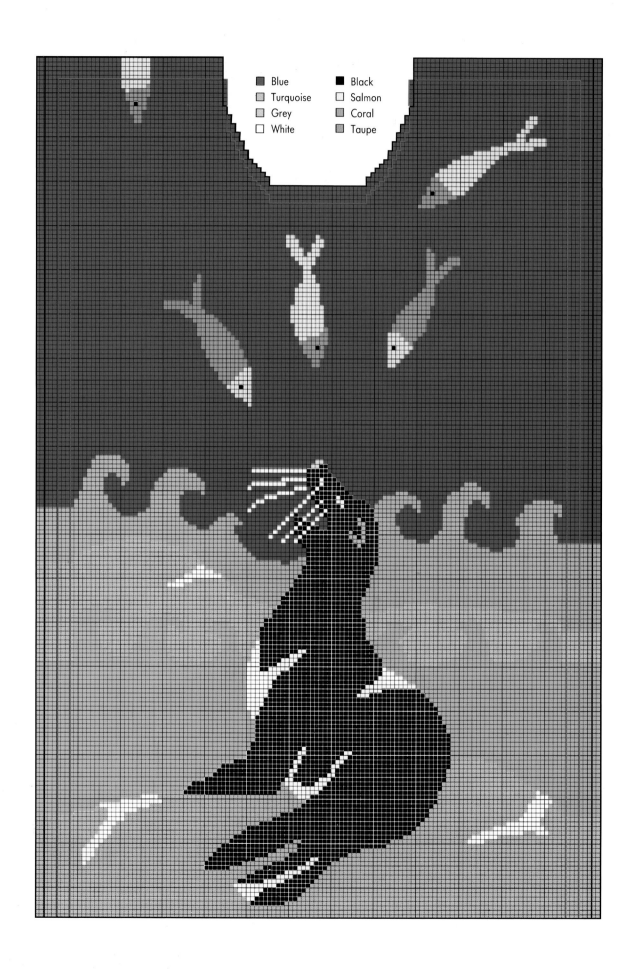

Blue
Turquoise
Grey
White
Black
Salmon
Coral
Taupe

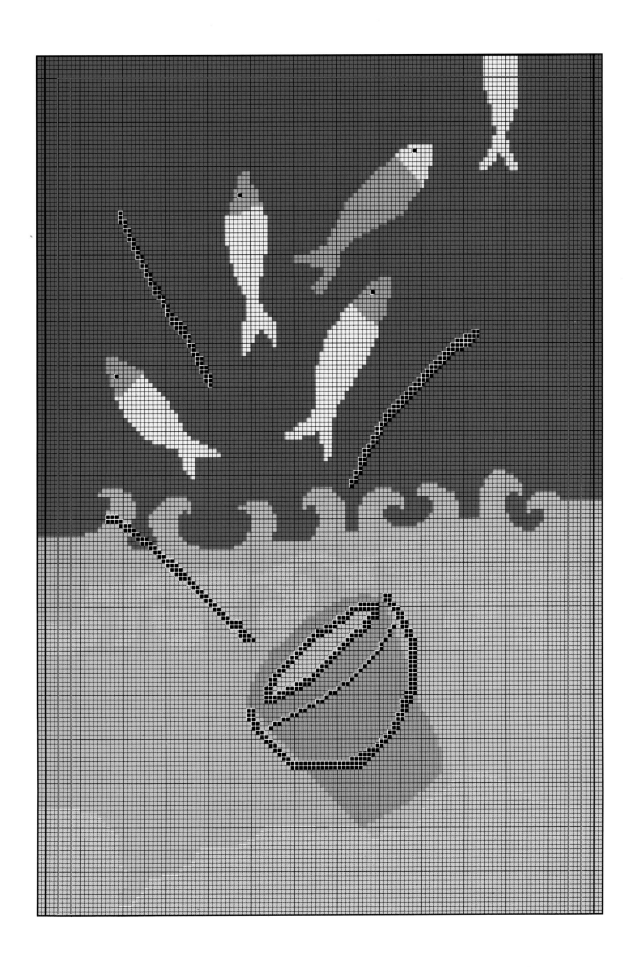

SEALED WITH A FISH

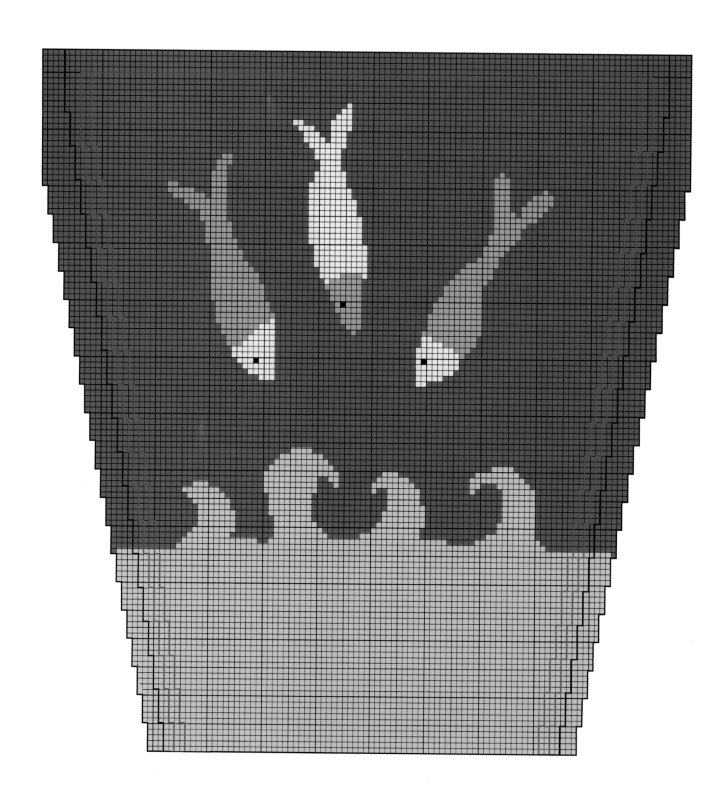

THE EYE OF THE TIGER

The design for this classic jacket was inspired by a Roman mosaic. It is worked in double-knitting wool using the intarsia method (see Techniques), and instructions are given for two sizes to fit chest sizes 102/112cm (40/44in).

BACK

Using 3¼mm needles and aubergine, cast on 148/160 sts and work in k2, p2 rib for 10cm (4in), inc 3/3 sts across last row of rib (151/163 sts).

Change to 4mm needles and begin following chart in st st until it is complete. Leave all sts on a spare needle.

LEFT FRONT

Using 3¼mm needles and aubergine, cast on 68/74 sts and work in k2, p2 rib for 10cm (4in), inc 3/3 sts evenly across last row of rib

(71/77 sts). Change to 4mm needles and begin following chart for left front to neck shaping. Next row (WS): cast off 6 sts at beg of this row and dec 1 st at same edge on the next 11 rows. Then dec 1 st at neck edge on following 4 alt rows (50/56 sts). Work without further shaping until chart is complete. Leave sts on a stitch holder.

RIGHT FRONT

Work as for left front, reversing all shapings – i.e., work rows from right to left in purl and from left to right in knit.

MATERIALS

Standard DK – 600gm aubergine; 100gm each of emerald, white and plum; 50gm each of brown, navy blue, red, burnt orange, barley, rust, slate, yellow and mustard. Short length of black. 7 buttons, 15mm (¾in) in diameter.

NEEDLES

One pair of 3¼mm needles and one pair of 4mm needles. Stitch holders.

TENSION

Using 4mm needles and measured over st st, 24 sts and 33 rows = 10cm (4in) square.

'Eye of the Tiger'
Classic double-knitting jacket with abstract tiger design.

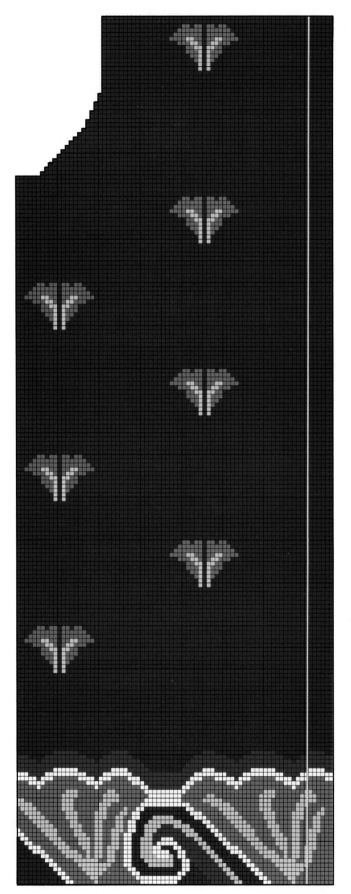

■ Aubergine
■ Emerald
□ White
■ Plum
▦ Brown
■ Navy
▦ Red
□ Burnt orange
□ Barley
▦ Rust
■ Slate
□ Yellow
□ Mustard
■ Black (for nose)

THE EYE OF THE TIGER

SLEEVES

(Both alike) Using 3¼mm needles and aubergine, cast on 46 sts. Work in k2, p2 rib for 7.5cm (3in), inc 17 sts evenly across last row of rib (63 sts). Begin following sleeve chart, inc 1 st at each end of every alt row until you have 111 sts, then inc 1 st at each end of every 4th row until you have 133 sts. Cont following chart without further shaping until it is complete. Cast off. With RSs of work facing each other, knit together the 50/56 sts from the front shoulders with the 50/56 sts from the back shoulders (51/51 sts remain at centre back neck).

NECKBAND

Using 3¼mm needles, aubergine and with RS facing, pick up and knit 37 sts up right front, 51 sts across back neck and 38 sts down left front (126 sts). Work in k2, p2 rib for 9cm (3½in). Cast off. Turn neckband inwards and slip stitch cast-off edge to pick-up edge.

BUTTONBAND

Using 3¼mm needles and aubergine, cast on 14 sts. Work in k2, p2 rib until band fits neatly to top of neckband when slightly stretched. With pins, mark positions for 7 buttons, the top button to be placed 3 rows down from the top and the bottom button 4 rows up from bottom, with the rest spaced evenly between.

BUTTONHOLE BAND

Work as for buttonband, making buttonholes as follows to correspond with positions of pins:
1st buttonhole row: rib 6, cast off 3, rib 5.
2nd buttonhole row: rib 5, cast on 3, rib 6.

MAKING UP

Sew sleeves to body, join side and sleeve seams. Sew buttonband neatly to left front and buttonhole band to right front. Sew on buttons.

THE EYE OF THE TIGER

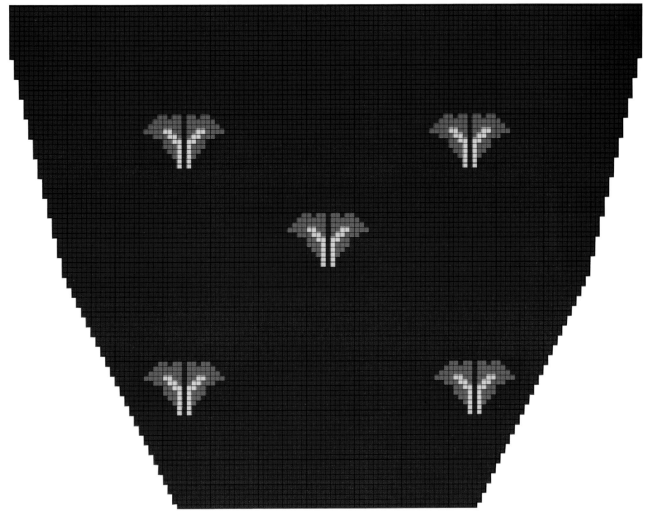

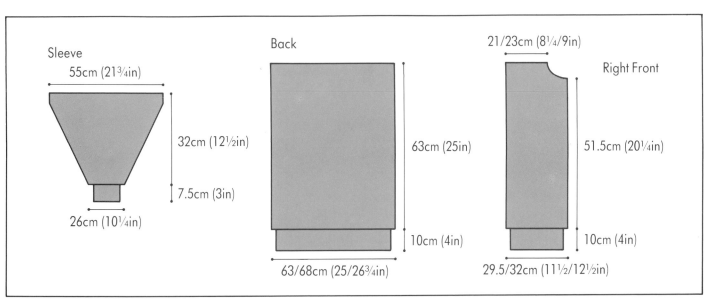

Sleeve
55cm (21¾in)
32cm (12½in)
7.5cm (3in)
26cm (10¼in)

Back
63cm (25in)
10cm (4in)
63/68cm (25/26¾in)

21/23cm (8¼/9in)
Right Front
51.5cm (20¼in)
10cm (4in)
29.5/32cm (11½/12½in)

SNAKE DANCE

A striking double-knitting cotton mix sweater, worked using the intarsia method (see Techniques). It will fit up to chest size 102cm (40in).

MATERIALS
DK cotton – 350gm black; 100gm green; 50gm each of yellow, red, turquoise, white, violet, fuchsia, coral and royal blue.

NEEDLES
One pair of 3¼mm needles and one pair of 4mm needles. Stitch holders.

TENSION
Using 4mm needles and measured over st st, 22 sts and 31 rows = 10cm (4in) square.

FRONT
Using 3¼mm needles and black, cast on 112 sts.
Row 1 (RS): p2, *sl 1, k2, psso, p2. Rep from * to end.
Row 2: k2, *p1, yrn, p1, k2. Rep from * to end.
Row 3: p2, *k3, p2. Rep from * to end.
Row 4: k2, *p3, k2. Rep from * to end.
Rep. these 4 rows 5 times more.
Next row (RS): knit this row, inc 19 sts evenly across it (13l sts).
Change to 4mm needles and begin following chart, working in st st without shaping until 140 rows are complete. **Shape neck:** k53, sl remaining sts on to a spare needle and, working on this first set of sts only, dec 1 st at neck edge on next row and the 9 following alt rows. Work straight until chart is complete. Leave remaining 43 sts on a holder. Slip centre 25 sts on to a stitch holder, rejoin yarn

to remaining sts and knit to end. Shape as for first side, then work straight until chart is complete. Keep remaining 43 sts on a stitch holder.

BACK
Work as for front following chart for back and ignoring neck shaping instructions. Work straight until chart is complete. Leave sts on a spare needle.

SLEEVES
(Both alike) Using 3¼mm needles and black, cast on 52 sts. Work in cable rib as for front for 24 rows. Next row: inc once into every st (104 sts).
Change to 4mm needles and work in st st until sleeve measures 36cm (14¼in) from start. Cast off loosely.
Knit left shoulder seam tog.

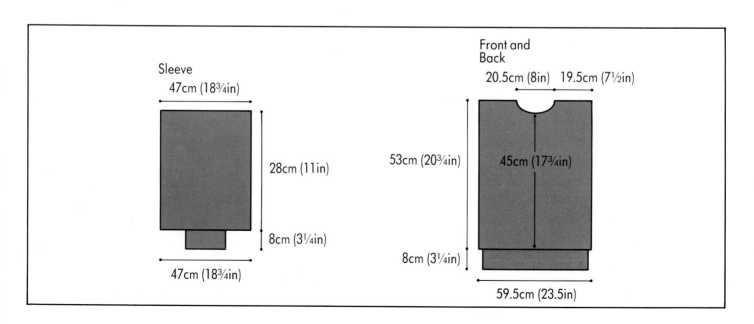

Sleeve
47cm (18¾in)

28cm (11in)

8cm (3¼in)

47cm (18¾in)

Front and Back
20.5cm (8in)   19.5cm (7½in)

53cm (20¾in)   45cm (17¾in)

8cm (3¼in)

59.5cm (23.5in)

SNAKE DANCE

Using 3¼mm needles and black, pick up and purl 26 sts down right side of neck, 25 sts from centre front, 26 sts up left side of neck, 45 sts across centre back (122 sts). Work in cable rib as for front for 5cm (2in). Cast off loosely in rib.

MAKING UP
Knit right shoulder seam together. Join sleeves to jumper, join side and sleeve seams, join neckband.

'Snake Dance'
Lady's black cotton jumper with python.

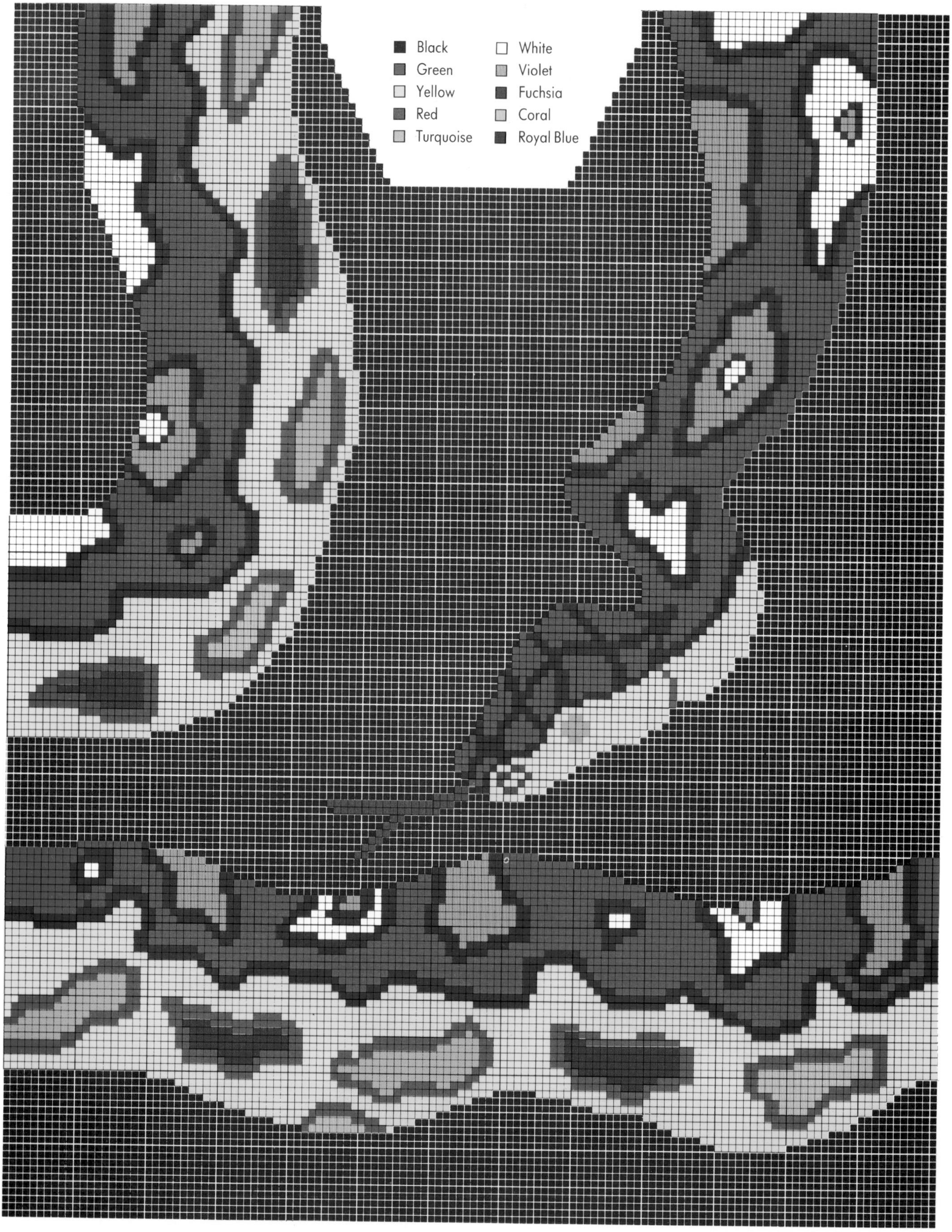
Black
Green
Yellow
Red
Turquoise
White
Violet
Fuchsia
Coral
Royal Blue

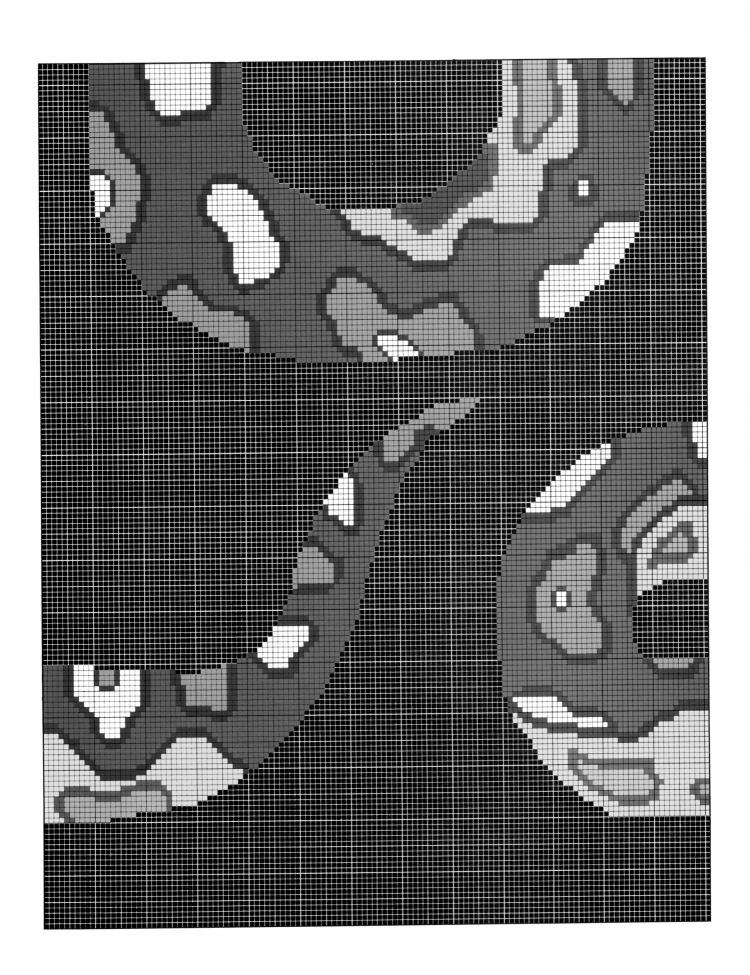

TREASURE ISLAND

This bright, chunky, one-size sweater is worked in stocking stitch, using the intarsia method (see Techniques). It will fit up to 96cm (38in) chest.

MATERIALS

Standard Chunky – 350gm yellow; 200gm turquoise; 150gm each of black and khaki; 50gm each of white, red, royal blue and mid-blue.

NEEDLES

One pair of 6mm needles. Stitch holders.

TENSION

Using 6mm needles and measured over st st, 14 sts and 20 rows = 10cm (4in) square.

BACK

Using 6mm needles and turquoise, cast on 72 sts and work in rib as follows:
Row 1: k2 turquoise, p2 yellow, rep to end.
Row 2: k2 yellow, p2 turquoise, rep to end.
Rep these 2 rows 18 times more.*
Change to st st and begin following chart, working straight until it is complete. Cast off 19 sts, place a coloured thread as a marker, cast off 34 sts, place a second thread and cast off remaining 19 sts.

FRONT

Work as for back to*.
Change to st st and begin working chart for front for 112 rows. **Shape neck:** next row: k26, leave remaining sts on a spare needle and, working on the first set of sts only, cast off 2 sts at beg of the next row and 1st at neck edge on the following 5 rows. Work 2 rows, cast off 19 sts. Slip centre 20 sts on to a holder, rejoin yarn to remaining sts and shape to match first side. Cast off remaining 19 sts.

RIGHT SLEEVE

Using 6mm needles and turquoise, cast on 36 sts and work in rib as for back for 16 rows.
Change to st st and commence following chart for sleeve, inc 1 st at each end of every 5th row until you have 64 sts. Work 12 rows straight. Cast off loosely.

LEFT SLEEVE

Work as for right sleeve but follow left sleeve chart.

NECKBAND

Using 6mm needles, turquoise and with RS of work facing, pick up and knit 9 sts down right front, 20 sts held for centre front, 9 sts up left front and 34 sts across centre back neck (72 sts). Work 20 rows in striped rib as for back. Cast off loosely.

MAKING UP

Join left shoulder seam. Turn neckband inwards and slip stitch cast-off edge to pick-up edge.
Using flat seams throughout, join sleeves to jumper and join side and sleeve seams.

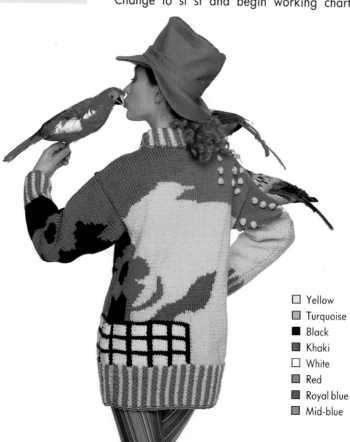

☐ Yellow
☐ Turquoise
■ Black
■ Khaki
☐ White
■ Red
■ Royal blue
☐ Mid-blue

$\otimes$ = make a bobble in yellow:
k4 from one, turn, p4, turn, k2 tog twice, turn, p2 tog

TREASURE ISLAND

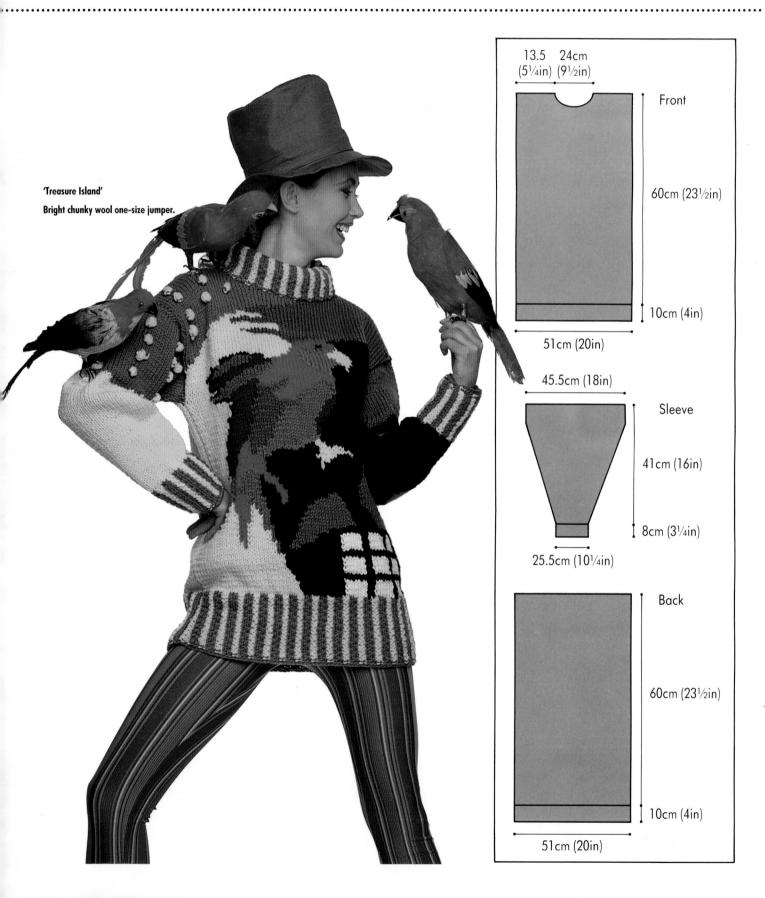

'Treasure Island'
Bright chunky wool one-size jumper.

13.5   24cm
(5¼in) (9½in)

Front

60cm (23½in)

10cm (4in)

51cm (20in)

45.5cm (18in)

Sleeve

41cm (16in)

8cm (3¼in)

25.5cm (10¼in)

Back

60cm (23½in)

10cm (4in)

51cm (20in)

TREASURE ISLAND

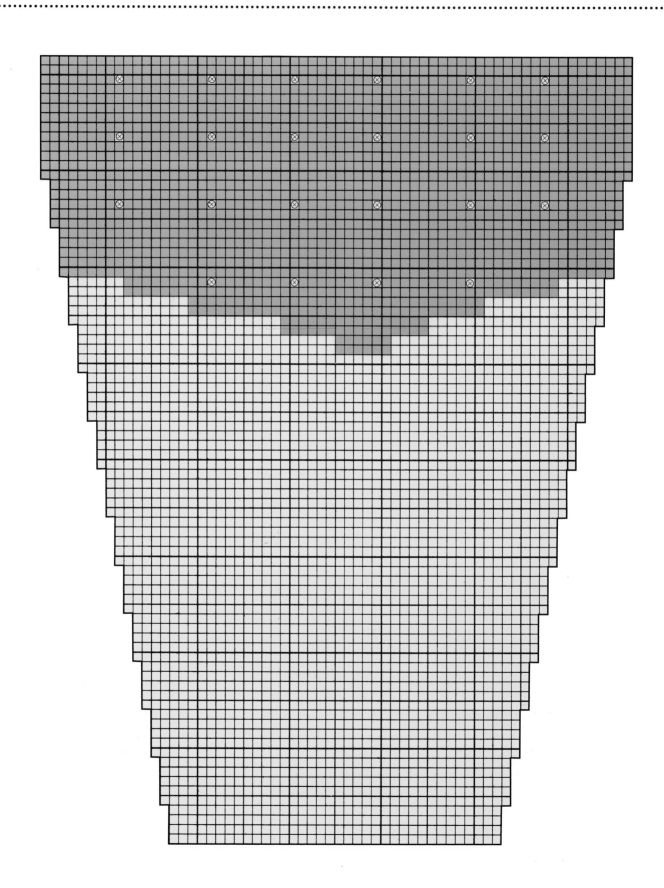

TREASURE ISLAND

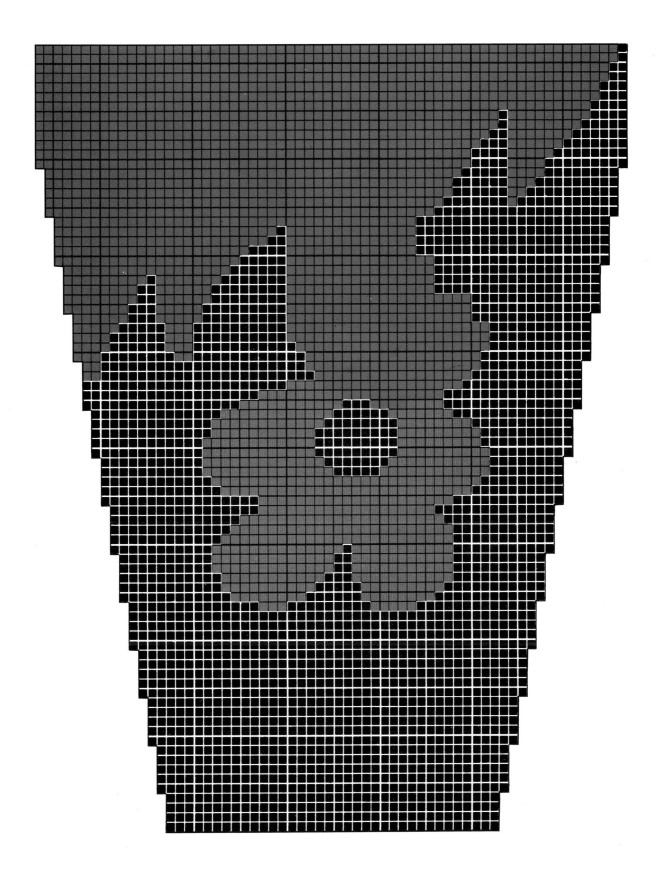

OUR FEATHERED FRIEND

This fun cotton T-shirt, which will fit up to 97cm (38in) chest, is worked in stocking stitch and loop stitch using the intarsia method (see Techniques).

LOOP STITCH
Knit rows only: hold third finger of left hand over yarn behind work, k1 (so that the yarn forms a loop around finger) but do not slip this stitch from needle; instead, transfer the stitch just worked back on to the left-hand needle and k2 through back loop (the stitch just knitted and the original stitch). Remove finger from the loop ready for next stitch. Make loops in the colour and position indicated on the chart.

FRONT
Using 3¾mm needles and green, cast on 88 sts and work in single rib for 10cm (4in), inc 12 sts evenly across last row of rib (100 sts). Change to 4½mm needles and begin following chart in st st, making loops as shown until 160 rows of chart have been worked. Work 6 rows in moss stitch in pink – i.e., row 1: k1. p1 to end. Row 2: p1. k1 to end. Rep these 2 rows twice more. Cast off.

BACK
Work as for front but follow chart for back.

SLEEVES
(Both alike) Using 3¾mm needles and green, cast on 68 sts and work in single rib for 5cm (2in), inc 4 sts evenly across last row of rib (72 sts).

Change to 4½mm needles and begin following chart for sleeves, inc 1st at each end of every 3rd row until you have 98 sts. Work 6 rows straight. Cast off loosely.

MAKING UP
Leaving a central neck opening of approximately 30cm (11¾in), join shoulder seams. Sew sleeves to body, sew side and sleeve seams.

'Our Feathered Friend Lady's loop stitch textured cotton jumper.

- ☐ Green
- ☐ Pink
- ■ Black
- ☐ Peach
- ☐ White
- ☐ Cream
- ☐ Yellow

x = make a
loop in white

(x) = make a
loop in black

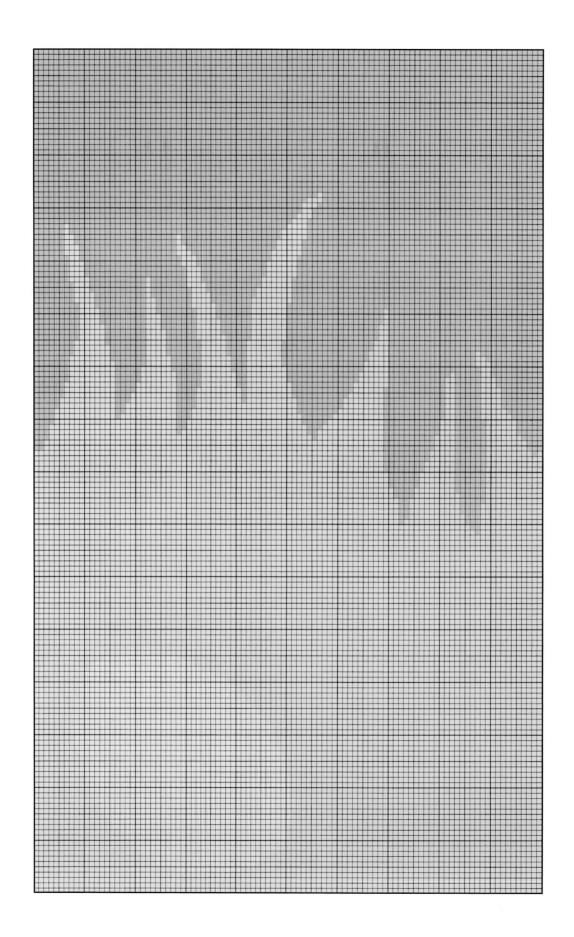

OUR FEATHERED FRIEND

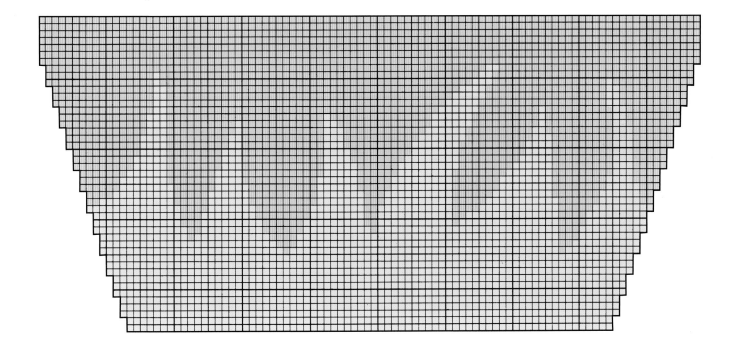

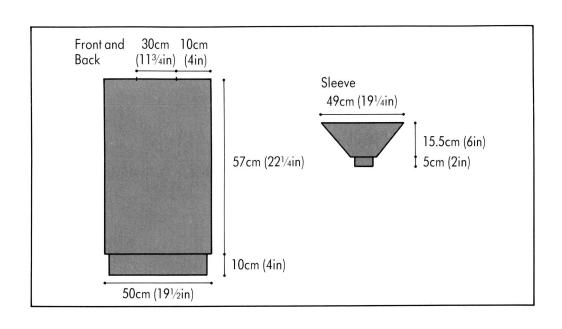

Front and Back

30cm (11¾in) 10cm (4in)

57cm (22¼in)

10cm (4in)

50cm (19½in)

Sleeve

49cm (19¼in)

15.5cm (6in)

5cm (2in)

'One Hump or Two?'
Lady's lumber jacket in chunky wool.

ONE HUMP OR TWO?

A lady's big butch jacket for desert nights, worked in chunky wool using the intarsia method (see Techniques).

BACK

Using 6mm needles and R, cast on 88 sts and work in garter st (knit every row) for 6 rows. Now work border stripes setting pattern as follows:

Row 1: k4R, k10Y, k10T, k10R, k10Y, k10T, k10R, k10Y, k10T, k4R.

Row 2: k4R, p10T, p10Y, p10R, p10T, p10Y, p10R, p10T, p10Y, k4R.

With sts thus set and keeping border of 4 garter sts at each end correct, rep these 2 rows 11 times more, then work row 1 once more (row 25 on chart has now been completed). Now, keeping chart correct and starting with a purl row, work rows 26-98 inclusive in st st. Cast off all sts in R.

RIGHT FRONT

Using 6mm needles and R, cast on 40 sts and work in garter st for 6 rows. Now work in border stripes, setting sts and colours as follows.

Row 1 (front edge RS): k10Y, k10R, k10T, k6Y, k4R.

Row 2: k4R, p6Y, p10T, p10R, p10Y.

Rep these 2 rows 11 times more, then rep first row once more. Now work in st st, beg with a purl row. Work rows 26-98 from chart. Cast off in R.

LEFT FRONT

Using 6mm needles and R, cast on 40 sts and work in garter st for 6 rows. Now work in border stripes, setting sts and colours as follows:

Row 1 (side edge RS): k4R, k6Y, k10T, k10R, k10Y.

Row 2: p10Y, p10R, p10T, p6Y, k4R.

Rep these 2 rows 11 times more, then rep first row once more. Now work in st st beg with a

MATERIALS

Standard Chunky – 400gm navy blue (N); 300gm rust (R); 150gm yellow (Y); 100gm turquoise (T); 50gm each of black (B) and camel (C). 9 buttons, 2.5cm (1in) in diameter.

NEEDLES

One pair of 5mm needles and one pair of 6mm needles. Stitch holders.

TENSION

Using 6mm needles and measured over st st, 14 sts and 20 rows = 10cm (4in) square.

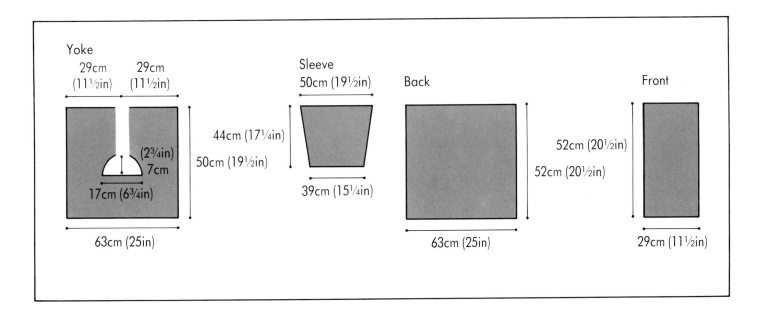

Yoke
29cm (11½in)   29cm (11½in)
(2¾in)
7cm
17cm (6¾in)
63cm (25in)

Sleeve
50cm (19½in)
44cm (17¼in)
50cm (19½in)
39cm (15¼in)

Back
63cm (25in)

Front
52cm (20½in)
52cm (20½in)
29cm (11½in)

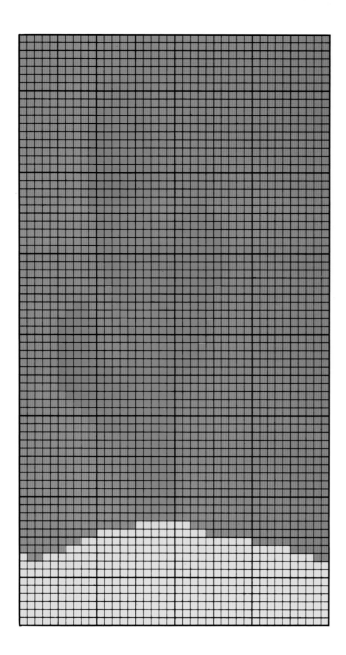

Navy blue
Rust
Yellow
Turquoise
Black
Camel

collar, knit to end in N. Now cont from chart for left front section, work 3 rows from chart, then inc 1 st at neck edge on next and every 3rd row twice, then on every alt row twice. Work 1 row, then cast on 3 sts at front edge on next row (40 sts). Keeping chart and garter st border correct, cont until row 94 has been worked. Work 6 rows in garter st in N on all sts. Cast off in N. Rejoin yarn to remaining sts and, keeping garter st border and chart correct, work to match first side.

SLEEVES

(Both alike) Using 6mm needles and R, cast on 54 sts and work in garter st for 6 rows. Now set border stripes as follows:

Row 1 (RS): k2R, k10Y, k10T, k10R, k10Y, k10T, k2R.

Row 2: p2R, p10T, p10Y, p10R, p10T, p10Y, p2R.

Rep these 2 rows 4 times more.

Row 11: inc into first st in R, k1R, k10Y, k10T, k10R, k10Y, k10T, k1R, inc into last st in R.

Row 12: p3R, p10T, p10Y, p10R, p10T, p10Y, p3R.

Row 13: k3R, k10Y, k10T, k10R, k10Y, k10T, k3R.

Rep these last 2 rows 3 times more, then row 12 again.

Row 21: inc into first st in R, k2R, k10Y, k10T, k10R, k10Y, k10T, k2R, inc into last st.

Row 22: p4R, p10T, p10Y, p10R, p10T, p10Y, p4R.

Row 23: k4R, k10Y, k10T, k10R, k10Y, k10T, k4R.

Rep these last 2 rows once more. Join in N and work 2 rows in st st. Now start chart section as follows:

Next row (knit): (11 sts from chart A, 12N) twice, 11 sts from chart A, 1N. With sts thus set, work 16 rows from chart, inc 1 st at each end of 3rd and 14th rows (62 sts).

Work 5 rows in st st in N.

Next row (purl): 14N, 11 sts from chart B,

purl row. Work rows 26-98 from right front chart, omitting the cactus. Cast off in R.

YOKE SECTION

(Starting at back yoke) Using 6mm needles and N, cast on 88 sts and work in garter st for 6 rows. Now cont in N, keeping first and last 3 sts on every row in garter st as a border. Cont from back and front yoke chart, starting at row 6. Work from chart until row 50 has been completed.

Row 51: k32N, sl next 24 sts on to a holder for

ONE HUMP OR TWO?

13N, 11 sts from chart B, 13N.
With sts thus set, work remaining 16 rows from chart, **at the same time**, inc 1 st at each end of the following 9th and 19th rows (**NB** increases come at each end of every 10th row throughout sleeve, 8 times in all). When both charts have been completed, cont in st st in N on these 66 sts for 5 rows.
Next row (purl): 5N, work 11 sts from chart A, 12N, work 11 sts from chart A, 12N, work 11 sts from chart A, 4N. With sts thus set, work 16 rows from chart, inc 1 st at each end of the next and following 10th row (70 sts). When charts have been completed, cont in st st in N for 3 rows, cast off in N.

BUTTONBAND

Using 5mm needles and R, cast on 8 sts and work in garter st until band fits neatly up from to beg of neck shaping when slightly stretched. Cast off. On this band mark positions for 9 buttons, the first to come on 3rd row, the last to come on 3rd row from cast off and the others spaced evenly between.

BUTTONHOLE BAND

Work as for buttonband, working buttonholes opposite marked positions as follows:
Buttonhole row 1: k3, cast off 2 sts, k to end.
Buttonhole row 2: k3, cast on 2 sts, k to end.

COLLAR

Join shoulder seams. Sew back and front yoke sections to body section. Pin front bands into place, easing to fit. Sew into place using a flat seam. Using 5mm needles, R and with RS facing, miss first 4 sts from buttonhole band, pick up and knit last 4 sts from buttonhole band and 3 sts from front neck edge, pick up and knit approximately 14 sts up right front neck, 24 sts from back neck stitch holder, approximately 14 sts down left front neck, 3 sts from front neck and 4 sts from buttonband (66 sts). Inc 8 sts evenly across

first row and work in garter st for 5cm (2in). Change to 6mm needles and cont in garter st until collar is 8cm (3¼in) deep. Cast off loosely.

MAKING UP

Set sleeves into place and sew cast-off body edges neatly along back and front yoke sections. Join sleeve seams and sew side

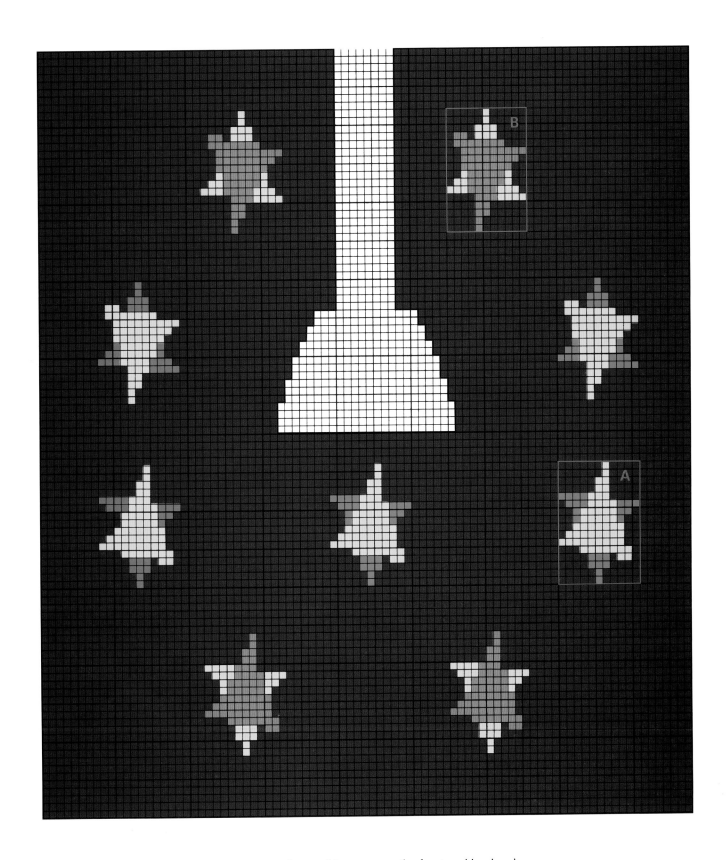

seams as far as garter st edges at sides. Sew on buttons to match buttonholes. Embroider camel's facial features in black as indicated on chart. Using alternate random colours, knot a fringe across the front and back yoke of jacket.

BAKED ALASKA

This smart Fair Isle and cable jumper is perfect for skiing. Worked in double-knitting wool, the snowflake motifs should be worked by the Fair Isle method, and the penguin itself should be worked using the intarsia method (see Techniques). The jumper will fit chest sizes 97/112cm (38/44in).

MATERIALS
Standard DK – 350gm white; 250gm each of red and black.

NEEDLES
One pair of 3¼mm needles and one pair of 4mm needles; 3 small cable needles; one short circular 3¼mm needle. Stitch holders.

TENSION
Using 4mm needles and measured over Fair Isle, 24 sts and 32 rows = 10cm (4in) square.

FRONT

Using 3¼mm needles and black, cast on 119/131 sts.

Row 1: (k1, p1) 13/16 times. Change to white, k6. Change to black, *(k1, p1) 12 times, k1. Change to white, k6. Rep from * once more. Change to black, (k1, p1) 12/15 times, k1.

Row 2: using black, p1, (k1, p1) 12/15 times. Change to white, p6. Change to black, *p1, (k1, p1) 12 times. Change to white, p6. Rep from * once more. Change to black, (k1, p1) 13/16 times. Rep the last 2 rows 4 times more.

Cable row: rib 26/32 as set. Change to white, cb6. Change to black, *rib 25 as set, cb6, rep from * once more. Change to black, rib as set to end. Rep rows 1 and 2 five times, rep cable row, working cf6 instead of cb6. Rep row 2 of rib as set. Next row: rib as set but inc 2/4 sts evenly across your first panel of plain black rib and 3/5 sts evenly across your last panel of plain black rib (124/140 sts).

Change to 4mm needles and begin following chart in st st, working snowflake motifs in Fair Isle and placing cables as indicated on the 11th and every following 10th row of chart. Work penguin motif using small separate balls of yarn for each area of colour. Cont without shaping until 150/168 rows have been worked. **Shape neck.** Next row: knit 54/62 sts from chart. Slip remaining sts on a holder and work on this first set of sts only. Cast of 5 sts at beg of next row, 3 sts at beg of the following alt row, 2 sts at beg of next 2 alt rows, then dec 1 st at neck edge on the next 4 alt rows. Work 9 rows without shaping. Cast off remaining 38/46 sts. Slip centre 16 sts on

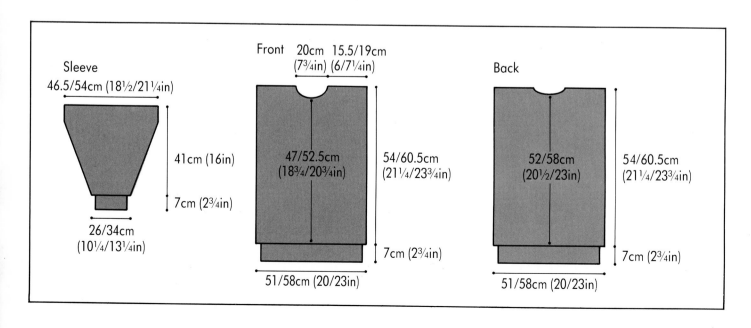

Sleeve
46.5/54cm (18½/21¼in)

41cm (16in)

7cm (2¾in)

26/34cm (10¼/13¼in)

Front   20cm   15.5/19cm
(7¾in)   (6/7¼in)

47/52.5cm (18¾/20¾in)

54/60.5cm (21¼/23¾in)

7cm (2¾in)

51/58cm (20/23in)

Back

52/58cm (20½/23in)

54/60.5cm (21¼/23¾in)

7cm (2¾in)

51/58cm (20/23in)

BAKED ALASKA

to a spare needle, rejoin yarn to remaining sts and k to end. Purl back to neck edge. Rep shaping as for other side of neck.

BACK

Work as for front (ignoring front neck shaping) until row 166/186 is complete. Continue following chart. **Shape neck.** Next row: k41/49 sts from chart. Leave remaining sts on a spare needle and, working on this first set of sts only, dec 1 st at neck edge on next 3 rows. Work 5 rows without shaping. Cast off remaining 46/46 sts. Slip centre 42 sts on to a stitch holder, rejoin yarn and knit to end. Dec 1 st at neck edge on next 3 rows. Work 5 rows without shaping. Cast off remaining sts.

SLEEVES

(Both alike) Using 3¼mm needles and black, cast on 53/63 sts.
Row 1: (k1, p1) 4/6 times. Change to white, k6. Change to black, (k1, p1) 12 times, k1. Change to white, k6. Change to black, (k1, p1) 4/7 times.
Row 2: using black, (k1, p1) 4/7 times. Change to white, p6. Change to black, p1, (k1, p1) 12 times. Change to white, p6. Change to black, (k1, p1) 4/6 times. Rep the last 2 rows 4 times more. **Cable row:** using black, rib 8/12 sts as set. Change to white, cb6. Change to black, rib 25 sts as set. Change to white, cb6, rib as set to end. Rep rows 1 and 2 five times. Rep cable row, working cf6 instead of cb6. Rep row 2 of rib as set. Next row: rib as set but inc 5/10 sts evenly across your first panel of plain black rib and 4/9 sts evenly across your last panel of plain black rib (62/82 sts).
Change to 4mm needles and begin following sleeve chart in st st, working cables as indicated on the 13th row and every following 10th row. **At the same time,** inc 1 st at each end of every 6th row 8/11 times, then every 4th row 16/13 times (112/130 sts).

'Baked Alaska'
His or hers jacquard skiing jumper with penguin panel.

BAKED ALASKA

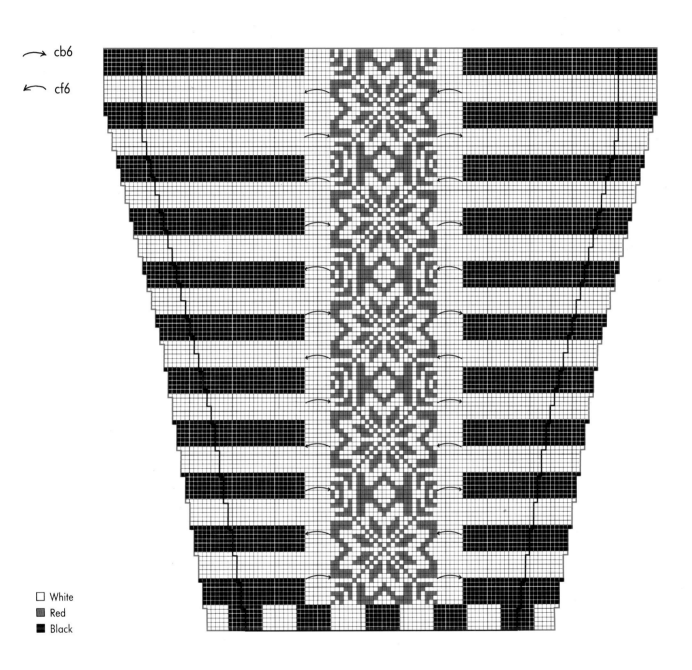

cb6

cf6

☐ White
◩ Red
■ Black

Work straight until chart is complete. Cast off loosely. Join shoulder seams.

NECKBAND

Using a 3¼mm circular needle and black, and starting with the 42 sts held for back neck, pick up and knit approximately 112/116 sts evenly around the neck. Work in k1, p1 rib for 8 rows, knit 1 row. Work 8 rows in rib and cast off loosely. Turn neckband inward and sl st cast-off edge to pick-up edge.

MAKING UP

Join sleeves to jumper, join side and sleeve seams, taking care to match stripes.

TAJ MAHAL

This bat-wing wrap-around top features Indian elephants in a festive mood. It will fit chest size 86-97cm (34-38in) and is worked in double-knitting yarn using the intarsia method (see Techniques). The sequins are added at the end.

MATERIALS
Standard DK – 550gm copper; 50gm each of camel, ecru, turquoise, gold, lilac, charcoal and bilberry. Coloured sequins.

NEEDLES
One pair of 3¼mm needles and one pair of 4mm needles.

TENSION
Using 4mm needles and measured over st st, 24 sts and 32 rows = 10cm (4in) square.

RIGHT FRONT/BACK

Using 4mm needles and copper, cast on 90 sts and, beginning with a knit row, follow the chart, working in st st for 2 rows. **Shape front:** keeping chart correct throughout, dec 1 st at beg of the next and every following alt row 15 times. Work 1 row.
Row 33 (RS): k2 tog, work from chart to last st, inc into this st.
Row 34: work from chart.
Keeping chart correct, rep sequence for inc and dec as set on these 2 rows 8 times more.

Shape sleeve

Row 51: k2 tog, work from chart to end, cast on 2 sts. Cont following chart, dec 1 st at neck edge on the next 11 alt rows and on the 20 following 3rd rows. **At the same time**, cast on 2 sts at the sleeve edge on the next 16 alt rows and 3 sts at the same edge on the following 9 alt rows. Work straight at armhole edge (cont neck decreases until they are complete) to row 138.
Row 139 (front edge): cast on 20 sts in ruby for centre back neck. Cont working straight until row 175 is complete.
Row 176 (WS): cast off 3 sts at beg of this row and the following alt row, then cast off 3 sts at beg of the next 7 alt rows and 2 sts at beg of the following 17 alt rows. Cast off 1 st at beg of the next 9 alt rows. Cont straight until chart is complete, cast off all sts.

LEFT FRONT/BACK

Work as for right front/back, reversing all shapings.

RIGHT FRONT BORDER AND TIE

Using 3¼mm needles and copper, cast on 17 sts for tie section and work as follows:
Row 1: sl 1, k15, k1 tbl.
Row 2: sl 1, p7, k1, p7, k1 tbl.
Rep these 2 rows until tie section measures 51cm (20in) ending with RS facing. Next row: cast off 9 sts, work to end, cast on 31 sts (39 sts).
Change to 4mm needles and work border section as follows. Next row (WS): sl 1, p14, k1, p13 from chart, p9, k1 tbl. Next row (RS): sl 1, k9, k13 from chart, k15, k1 tbl. With sts thus set, cont rep chart until border section (39 sts) fits neatly along cast-on sts of right front. Cast off.

LEFT FRONT BORDER AND TIE

Using 3¼mm needles and copper, cast on 17 sts and work rows 1-2 from right front border and tie until work measures 91.5cm (36in), ending with WS facing. Cast off 9 sts, work to end, cast on 31 sts (39 sts).
Change to 4mm needles and work as follows. Next row (RS): sl 1, k15, k13 from chart, k9, k1 tbl.
Next row (WS): sl 1, p9, p13 from chart, k1, p14, k1 tbl. With sts thus set, cont until work fits neatly along left front cast-on sts. Cast off all sts.

BACK BORDER SECTION

Using 4mm needles and copper, cast on 39 sts and work as follows:
Next row (starting at right back edge, RS): sl 1, k9, k13 from chart, k15, k1 tbl. Next row: sl 1, p14, k1, p13 from chart, p9, k1 tbl. Rep this

'Taj Mahal'
Lady's crossover cardigan with sequins.

sequence until border fits neatly along back cast-off sts (both sections of back).

MAKING UP AND FRONT EDGING

On right front, fold border section in half at hem-line and catch stitch into place on wrong side without pulling seam. Sew left front border section to match. Using a flat seam, sew border sections into place along cast-on edges of right and left fronts. Now work rib front band as follows: using 3¼mm needles and copper, cast on 8 sts and work as follows:

Next row: sl 1, (k1, p1) 3 times, k1 tbl.

Rep this row until band fits neatly up front shaped edge from hem row on border to finish at centre back neck when slightly stretched. Cast off in rib.

Work left front band to match.

Neatly sew centre back seam. Using a flat seam, sew bands into place along front edges, easing to fit and placing behind tie sections. Join with a flat seam at centre back neck.

Sew sequins in the centre of each small motif.

SLEEVE CUFFS

Using 4mm needles, ruby and with RS facing, pick up and knit 70 sts along sleeve edge. Starting with a purl row, work in st st for 8 rows. Cast off evenly. Turn cuff to inside and sl st into place. Fold border sections back in half at hem-line and catch stitch into place on wrong side. Sew into place along back cast-off sts using a flat seam. Sew sleeve and side seams. On right-hand side seam, leave a gap for tie to go through. Fold ties in half at hem-line and sew along bottom and cast-on edges. Neatly finish all ends.

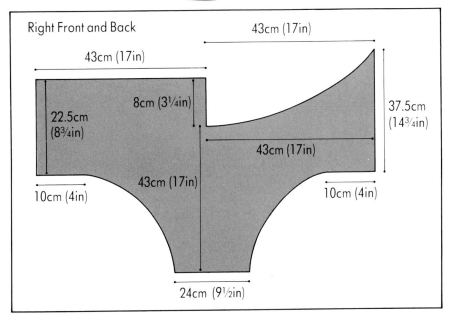

Right Front and Back

43cm (17in)

43cm (17in)

8cm (3¼in)

22.5cm (8¾in)

37.5cm (14¾in)

43cm (17in)

43cm (17in)

10cm (4in)

10cm (4in)

24cm (9½in)

TAJ MAHAL

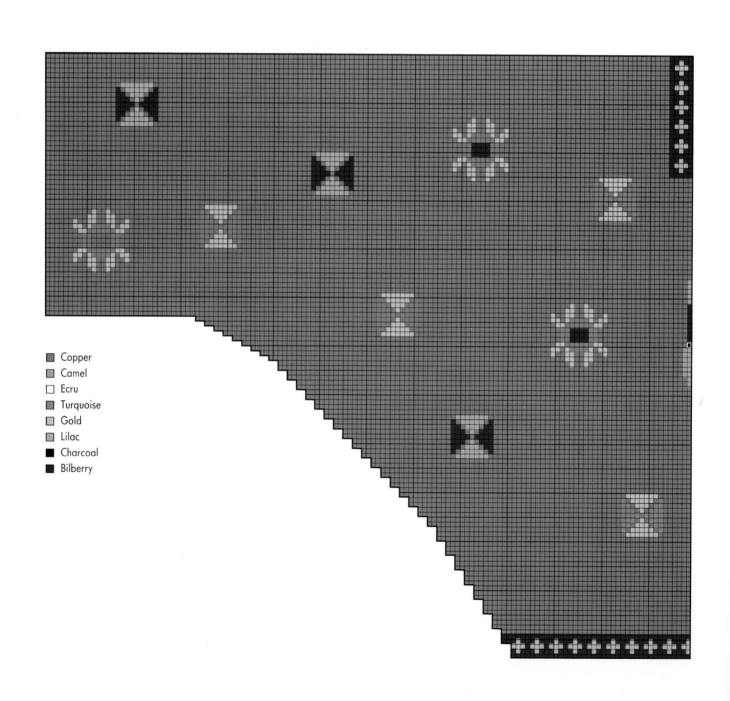

- ■ Copper
- ■ Camel
- □ Ecru
- ■ Turquoise
- ■ Gold
- ■ Lilac
- ■ Charcoal
- ■ Bilberry

TAJ MAHAL

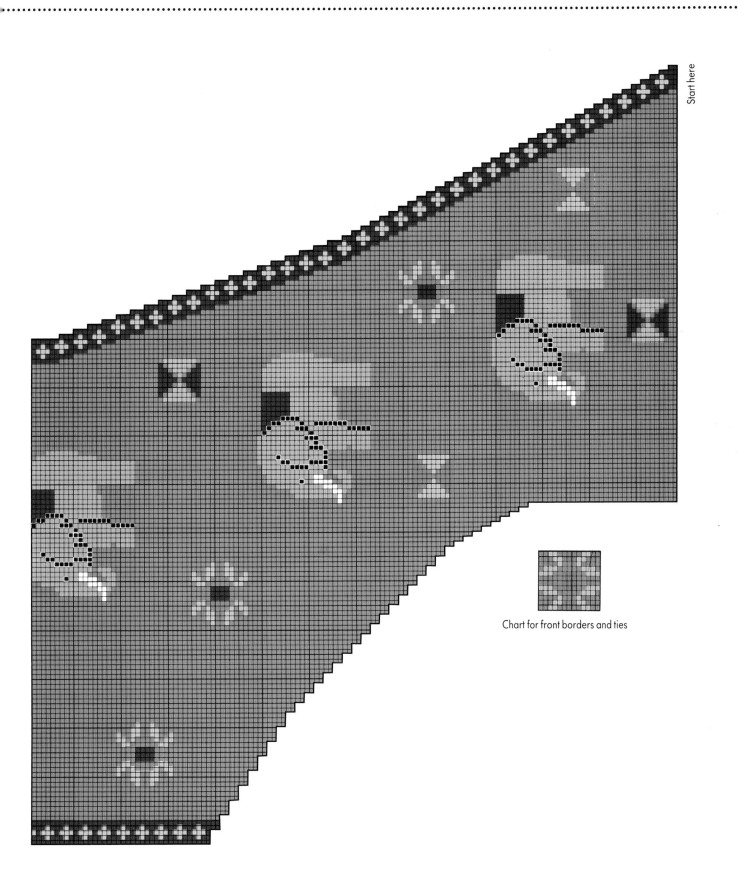

Start here

Chart for front borders and ties

CREDITS

Covent Garden General Store (inflatables); Cutler & Gross (glasses); Escapade (cat suit and gold mask); Hamleys (soft animals); Kathryn Hamnett (seal leggings); The Hat Shop (hats); Hyper Hyper (snake dance and Taj Mahal leggings); Cornelia James (gloves); Johnsons (men's shoes and leather trousers); Lawtex (umbrellas); Mary Quant (tights and leggings); Neal Street East (fake birds, snake basket, flute, fish, pineapples and wooden lilies); Next B&G (kids' outfits); Shellys (women's shoes); and Chrissie Walsh (giraffe shorts and Treasure Island leggings).

Photography	Liz McCauley
Styling	Bo Chapman
Make-up	Judith Pallen
Models	Justine Coss (Laraine Ashton), Matt Holland (Models 1) and Abigail McDonald (Premier)
Design	Heather Johns

YARN INFORMATION

Most of the yarns listed in this book are of a standard weight and knit to a standard tension. However, required amounts may vary depending on whether you select pure wool, cotton, or a synthetic mix. The weights listed are for a 50 per cent/50 per cent natural fibre and acrylic mix. If you are using pure wool, add approximately 50gm to the weight of the main colour, and for pure cotton add approximately 100gm. If you have any difficulty obtaining the correct colours, you can mix and match yarns from brand to brand; just ensure that all your selected yarns knit to the same standard tension.

Designs knitted in Melinda Coss yarns are available in kit form. For details write to:

Melinda Coss Knitting
Ty'r Waun Bach
Gwernogle
Dyfed
West Wales
SA32 7RY
Tel: 0267 202 386

For details on Wendy yarns write to:

UK	*USA*
Carter & Parker Ltd.	Berroco Inc.
Gordon Mills	Elmdale Road
Guiseley	PO Box 367
West Yorkshire	Uxbridge
LS20 9PD	MA 01569
Tel: 0943 872264	Tel: 508-278-2527